BLOOD IS THICKER THAN COLOR

TJ Morris

ISBN-13: 978-1502781789
ISBN-10: 1502781786

Table of Contents

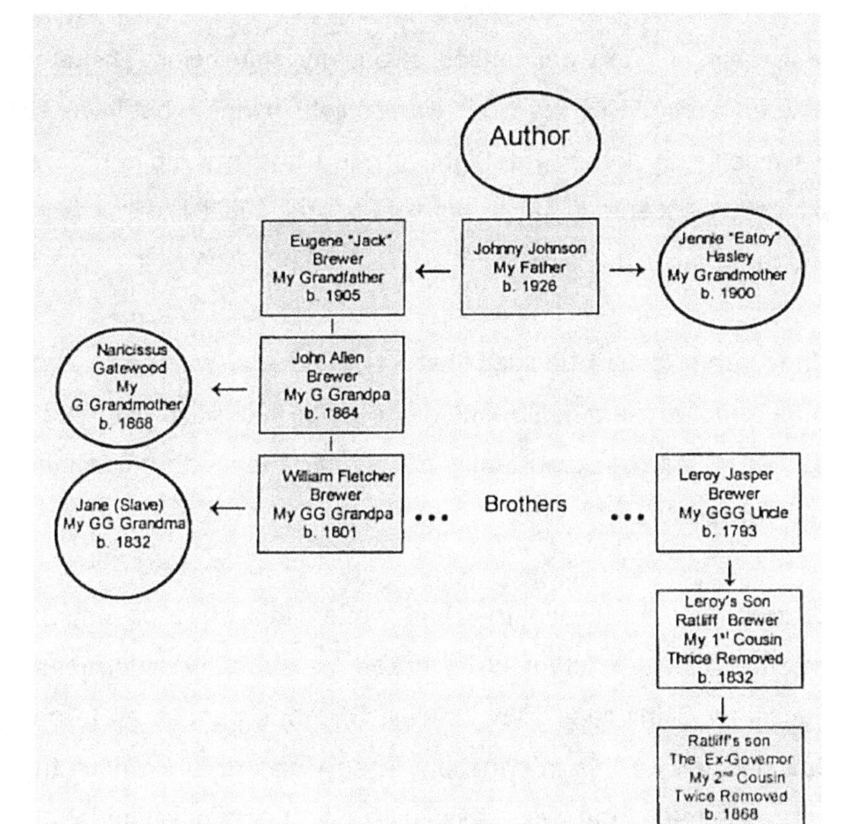
Author
Eugene "Jack" Brewer My Grandfather b. 1905
Johnny Johnson My Father b. 1926
Jennie "Eatoy" Hasley My Grandmother b. 1900
Naricissus Gatewood My G Grandmother b. 1868
John Allen Brewer My G Grandpa b. 1864
Jane (Slave) My GG Grandma b. 1832
William Fletcher Brewer My GG Grandpa b. 1801
Brothers
Leroy Jasper Brewer My GGG Uncle b. 1793
Leroy's Son Ratliff Brewer My 1st Cousin Thrice Removed b. 1832
Ratliff's son The Ex-Governor My 2nd Cousin Twice Removed b. 1868

Preface

As a child, I often got teased about my skin color. The other children wanted to know why I was so light skinned, but I was still *Black folk*. My father was light skinned and my mother brown skinned. I accepted that I was light skinned just like my father and these were the facts.

Many years later, I decided that I needed and wanted to know more about my family. So, one day during Black History Month of 2007, I pulled out some family history information that my father had passed on.

Actually, I was the one that had written this story on paper. I didn't recall this, until my sister asked me about this information. Our father didn't read or write well. She was curious as to how Dad had left us this information. Then I was able to recall that Dad had made me write this information, while sitting at the kitchen table. This is why it was in cursive and print. It also had *several* misspelled words. I had to have been about nine years old, when Dad made me take dictation. He was making me practice my handwriting and my spelling, while he tried to drill the family history into me, but I wasn't interested. I do remember that he wasn't much help with the spelling either.

I had read this family information several times in the past, since the passing of my father in 1987. I had even translated some of this information into an American Sign Language for a homework assignment, but after the assignment was over, it was returned to its proper storage place.

The most memorable part of this information for me was the mentioning of a *Governor* and that this man was somehow related to us. Well, now I wanted to know who he was and how this Governor was related?

This was the beginning of a seven year genealogy voyage that has led to the telling of this story. I always knew the main part of the story. Just about everyone in my family knows the tale of my grandfather (Jack Brewer) and his *adventure with the law*, which is the story that I have chosen to share.

I always wondered what Dad left me when he died. He left me this story...

Acknowledgments

There are so many people that have made a contribution to this book that I dare not try to name them all, for fear that I may leave someone out, but I will name a few.

I especially thank my husband Reginald Morris and my daughter Taryn Morris for supporting me during my creative endeavors of this book. Secondly, I would like to thank my mother Louise Johnson and my sister Therese Johnson for their unconditional love. Thirdly, I want to thank the Brewer family and a special thanks to my cousins Vanessa Brewer-Allen, D. Miles Davis and James Cobbins for their contributions of some key points.

I'm appreciative and thankful to Cynthia Hogan for accompanying me to Mississippi on my genealogy quest and the Kenosha Writer's Guild for helping me with my writing. I'm also thankful for the wonderful editors that I was able to get assistance from, Michelle Thomas and Derotha Rogers. Big thanks to my cover designer Barbara Murphy of Murphy Design.

Lastly, I would like to thank Harold Smith for starting and administrating the Carroll County Mississippi Genealogy online group, where he answered many questions for me and I was able to meet Tavon Pugh who contributed the Foreword.

I had many unanswered questions when I started writing this story, but due to my Buddhist practice and wonderful responses from the universe, I was able to connect with people, rekindle family ties and meet many members of my family that I knew nothing of. I am grateful.

Foreword

My name is Tavon Pugh and I'm from Washington, D.C. Genealogy has always been important to my family, and me especially, for as long as I've known. In my family, there are plenty of tragedies, love stories, scandals, betrayals, racism, and a bunch of crazy people.

One of my favorite stories in my family history is the event that took place at an old church in the Hills of Carroll County, Mississippi at Rosebank Methodist Baptist Church, in Coila Mississippi. This event took the life of a newly-wed young woman that they called "Honey", my great-great-great-great Aunt Alma Lark-Jordan. As the story goes (based on different accounts, they all pretty much have the same information), there was a convention, or gathering, at the church with the people of the town in attendance. As I'm told, fish and homemade ice cream was on the menu, and my aunt Alma must have had a little bit too much ice cream, because she began complaining of having stomach aches. She left out of the church to go use the bathroom when all of a sudden, a shootout broke out between the local sheriff of BlackHawk, and a civilian Mr. Eugene "Jack" Brewer, who was nearly as white as the sheriff.

Alma was supposed to have been shot right through her heart, and another source also says that she was hit on the head with something heavy. I don't know what, but she definitely died on that day. A woman from the area was in attendance with her boyfriend.

She told an elder cousin of mine in Chicago, what she could remember, and this is that someone had gone up to the church window to inform Alma's mother, Mahalia "Mahaly" McGlothin-Lark-Stanley (my 3rd great grandmother), of the tragic incident. She was said to have jumped up from the pew and cried, "They killed my Alma."

Not much is known about Aunt Alma. She never had any children, but her husband, Mr. Albert "Fonzie" Jordan has several living descendants with his second wife. Some of these descendants and their children still reside in Carroll County, MS.

There aren't too many people who can recall anything about aunt Honey, but the one physical description that we have of her is that she was a heavy set woman.

Evidently, the families must have forgotten about this tragic event, because there have been several marriages between these two families. Today, these two families live amongst each other out in the Hills of Carroll County, with the story of this tragic event from the 1920's, long forgotten.

Tavon M. Pugh

Author's Note

I have a story to tell.

Earl Leroy Brewer was the thirty-eighth Governor of Mississippi. He was also my grandfather's second cousin. This made him my second cousin, twice removed, on my dad's side of the family. My grandfather's grandpa and the Ex-Governor's grandpa were brothers.

For most of my life, I thought these men were Irish; but after my own DNA test and genealogy search, I learned that they were not. I also learned that I am 27.69% European (Finnish, Orcadian and Russian) and 72.31% West African/Yoruba.

My grandpa's name was Eugene “Jack” Brewer. His grandfather was William Fletcher Brewer. Around 1848, William went to Tennessee to buy a sixteen-year-old mulatto, domestic slave girl named Jane. Jane was described as having long beautiful hair--long enough for her to sit on--as she rode on a horse that trailed behind William on their journey back to Mississippi.

William depended on Jane to cook, clean, and nurse him back to health when he became sick. During that time he would cry out, *“It's all hell in my throat.”* As it turned out, she wasn't just a domestic servant and nurse. Jane was also his mistress with whom he fathered five children. Jane and their children lived in a home on Williams' land. My great grandpa *John Allen Brewer* was one of these children and Eugene "Jack" Brewer's father.

After William died in 1874, the authorities came to the house and forced Jane to open the strongbox, where people usually housed their important papers and valuables, such as bonds, gold, deeds to land and promissory notes, etc., for safekeeping. The authorities stole everything that was in the strongbox, leaving Jane and her children with little or nothing. Shortly after, Jane married a Negro man named Mr. Cox.

Governor Brewer was born in 1868, and my great grandfather was born four years earlier. My grandfather was born in 1905, all in Carroll County Mississippi. A relationship did exist between Great Grandpa John Allen Brewer and the Ex-Governor Earl Leroy Brewer, but one that did not permit play or even acknowledgment of family ties. This relationship of separation may have become a major contributing factor to the wonderful compassion that Ex-Governor Earl Leroy showed for people of color.

This is the story I have to tell, a family story about my Grandfather and what his cousin the former Governor of Mississippi, Earl Leroy Brewer, did for him in the 1920's.

This is a story of struggles and acceptance and survival.

Chapter 1

It was a warm day in March 1926. In the South, this was not unusual weather. The tranquility of the afternoon was interrupted when gunshots erupted into the streets of Carroll County Mississippi. Shocking screams of the panicky pedestrians added to the blaring of chaos as people dodged bullets and ran for cover. In the aftermath, a woman lay dead in the streets, killed in the crossfire, and the sheriff had a gunshot wound in his left arm. The shooter, a mulatto, managed to get away, but he quickly landed the top position on the sheriff's "Most Wanted" list.

In his escape, the shooter's heart pounded through his eardrums; he knew he had to make his way up North. He had to get out of the South if he was to survive. At twenty-one years old and average build, the shooter was a good-looking young man – *with a bounty on his head.* He became a man on the run through the backwoods, swamps and the cotton fields of Mississippi, all the while thinking and planning how to save his life. How would he make it up North without being caught?

He knew that the laws of the South would not allow him to be a passenger on the train, but perhaps he could sneak into and hide inside a boxcar. The authorities and possibly a mob of angry white men were looking for him. He was an *outlaw* and most of all – a *nigger.* His heart pumped faster than ever. This man was *Eugene Brewer,* better known as *Jack.*

This young man's skin was as fair as they come, but he had that *drop* of black blood that labeled him a Negro and Southern society treated him as such. Nothing in his appearance said this man was a Negro, but people who knew him knew his race. Remember this was during the time of segregation and every Negro had a place.

The sweat poured down his body and his breath blew out in spurts. Jack ran until he could run no more. His chest heaving with every gulp of air, he fell on his hands and knees to the ground. All of a sudden he heard a woman's voice singing a song. Following the sound, Jack saw a slightly thin, brown skinned Negro woman of average height with medium length hair. There wasn't anything special about her appearance.

Walking closer, Jack saw that the woman was working, scrubbing clothes and hanging them in the yard to dry. As he approached, "Jack" caught her attention.

Living in a small, secluded wooden shack located about a half mile off the main road, Jennie didn't get many visitors. While she recognized him as a familiar face, she sensed that something had to be wrong to bring Jack by her way. She called out to him.

"Hey, your'ra Brewer boy, ain't cha?"

Jack, whisking away the sweat burning his eyes and attempting to catch his breath, pushed the words out in short gasps, "I sure could use somethin' tuh drank."

"Don't you have some bruders?"

"Yep, I's got brothers. My name Jack."

"My name Jennie. Let's go in and get somethin' tuh drank and you can rest a spell. You's look like yuh might be running from dat dhere Sheriff. What you done did?"

Jennie waved and called to her children to come into the house as she and Jack walked toward her house, which was in need of some repairs. Jack took notice of the loose stair-boards as he stepped onto the porch with a large rocking chair.

Stepping into the house, Jennie and Jack came into one large room, which included the cooking space. Two smaller rooms were positioned behind the larger room. Looking at his surroundings, Jack saw that the rooms were almost bare of non-essentials, no accessories like curtains and wallpaper. Two black cast iron skillets lined one wall, along with rough hewn shelves that held the homemade preserves. Almost all the windows were dull and cloudy, and wooden boards across another window formed an X, making it perfect for Jack. One could see very little when looking through the windows into or outside of the house. As far as Jack was concerned, this was a perfect hideout. He was glad that no one could see straight in. A square wooden table stood in the middle of the room with three wooden chairs. A fourth chair with a broken leg sat in a corner. The outhouse stood about a hundred feet from the main house.

Jack did spot a portrait next to a radio on top of a dresser in the largest room. Gazing at the photo more closely, he saw Jennie, her three children and a man that Jack assumed to be her husband. The sight of Jennie in the photo made Jack realize that he knew her, that he had met Jennie several years ago at a family gathering when they were younger. Now Jack had grown to be a man, they had both married and Jennie had three children. He remembered that Jennie was a few years older than he.

Meanwhile, Jennie prepared slices of egg pie and cups of cold cider to serve as she and Jack became reacquainted. When Jack didn't see the man of house anywhere, he inquired. "Where yo husband Ma'am?"

Jennie bowed her head, closed her eyes to hold back a tear, and said softly, "He be on the chang."

Considering the possibility of his own fate, Jack quickly changed the subject and complimented Jennie on her egg pie which was known to be some of the finest egg-pie in Carroll County.

Jennie was a lonely woman whose husband had been on the chain for several months. He would be released soon, but Jennie longed for male companionship. Jack stayed the night with Jennie, who washed his clothing and gave him some of her husband's things, although somewhat large for Jack. Of course they would have to do, taking into account his own situation.

Jack continued to worry that the authorities were still searching for him with the dogs and the Klan, so he and Jennie talked through the night as Jack waited for the Sheriff's search to die down. Eventually, he told her why he was on the run.

Singing and dancing the next day, Jennie cooked breakfast for Jack and her children. She was so happy to have some male company and they continued to talk most of the morning.

"Always sanging in the morning?" Jack asked.
"Be lak dat after a good night sleep."

"I's had a good night sleep too. I's thank you for lettin' me spen' the night. When's the mis'ta coming home?"

"He be round bout dis way in a couple mo weeks." Jennie asked, "You's coming back dis way?"

Jack answered with conviction, "If I survive, I'm never coming back. I's can't never come back dis way. Dat sheriff and ever'other white man in Carroll County dead set on strangin' me up, if giv'n the chance. He done probably put out a warrant to pinch me. I's bess get out the South."

"Don't worry. He got tuh tend tuh dat arm you done put a plug in."

But Jack knew deep in his soul that a bullet in the arm would not prevent the white men from carrying out their manhunt. That bullet was the motivator that propelled their mission to murder.

Chapter 2

Jack left Jennie's home noontime the next day with some reluctance, but his urge to survive overwhelmed any unwillingness to leave. To cover his getaway, Jack trudged back to his papa's land in BlackHawk from Jennie's home, which was also in BlackHawk, through the cotton and corn fields. He was determined to get away from his hunters. He hoped to hop into a boxcar on a train in Greenwood after obtaining a ride.

Greenwood was several miles north. The breeze rustled through the stalks of plants and vegetables, as he made his way back to the Brewer family home. No one detected Jack's movement through the swaying vegetation.

Nearing his papa's house, Jack saw his stepbrother Norman working in the fields.

"Pssst! Pssst!......Norman"

Norman turned in the direction of the sound of his name. In a voice of anxious concern and surprise, he whispered, "Jack, What you doing here?"

"I's need you tuh take me tuh the train," Jack spoke as softly as he could.

“Okay, I'll meet you at the barn.” Norman dropped his tools and ran to the house collecting any cash that he could for Jack. Riding in their papa’s Model T Ford (Jack’s family were not poor Negroes. His father owned enough land to buy several Model T’s), Jack scrunched down in the back seat and suffered the rough ride while Norman drove his brother through the uneven, dirt paths of Mississippi’s rutted back roads to the train yard in Greenwood.

During the trip, Norman questioned his brother, “We heard what happened at church yesterday. Everybody pretty upset. Where you stay last night? Heard dat Sheriff might lose his arm.”

“I's stayed at Jennie Johnson's. When she recognized me, she invited me in. She saw dat I needed some help. Her husband on the chain.”

They continued their conversation until Norman dropped Jack off in the yard. Jack was ready to hop a ride on a freight train, but as he approached the yard, he spotted two workers having a smoke. Jack also caught a sight of an open boxcar, but to get to the boxcar, he had to pass the workers. The one thing that Jack had in his favor was his fair complexion. Jack had the skin color of a white man. Hoping that the men had not heard the news, Jack held his head down, tipped his hat and nodded politely as he passed the workers. These men didn't think much of seeing Jack in the yard, because white folks were always cutting through the train yard on their way to the main part of town or to catch a passenger train. When the engineer called out to these two men, he gave Jack the distraction that he needed, the chance to climb into the open boxcar, the opportunity to get out of Mississippi and the good fortune to survive.

"Hey, Bob, Larry, come here for a minute."

Inside the boxcar were bales of cotton where Jack quickly found a spot, where he couldn't be seen. He knew that workers would be locking this car shortly.

After several hours, the train came to a long stop. The atmosphere in the locked boxcar had risen to extremely high temperature. Panting heavily, Jack suffered, as if he would die of thirst with sweat pouring down his face. Since the train had not moved in twenty minutes, Jack thought he would try to get off the train.

Jack stood by the door listening for any possible sounds and thought how he would exit the train. He had to flip the latch that was on the outside of the car with little space in the area where the boxcar locked; he would have to use an old pitchfork that was left in the boxcar. Jack grabbed the fork and tried to open the door as delicately as he could. He struggled with the pitchfork and the lock. The bales of cotton didn't leave room in the boxcar for Jack to maneuver. All of a sudden, the door flew open and the pitchfork went flying back into the cotton. Jack fell out of the car and landed face first in the dirt near the tracks. At this moment, the engineer spotted him and called out.

"Hey You! What you doing over there?"

Jack got up quickly and took off running into a woody area with tall grasses, weeds and trees, providing the perfect place for Jack to disappear into thin air. He left the engineer scratching his head and wondering where he went. "I thought I just saw somebody; where'd he go? I must be working too hard."

Once Jack was able to come out of the grassy, woody area, he spotted a road sign, indicating that he was in Caruthersville, MO. He saw a familiar landmark, one he had seen on several occasions. Jack knew that his uncle lived approximately eight miles from where the train stopped. If he could just make it to his uncle's home, Jack would be able to rest, bathe and possibly get some assistance. Feeling the light breeze of warm air, Jack walked the short distance to the main street, the heart of town. Compared to the smoldering freight car, the warm breeze cooled Jack's skin enough to evaporate the drenching sweat.

A number of town folk mingled in and out of the storefront businesses on this street: a barbershop, an ice cream parlor, a drug store and a few other buildings. One man was getting his shoes shined outside the barbershop. This was about all this town had to offer.

A few people took notice of the stranger walking onto the main street, a new face in town. This realization made Jack quickly pull down the brim of his cap to partially cover his face. After all, he was still in the South, and he was still a man on the run. Taking no chances with that Sheriff, Jack decided it would be best to get off the main street. He continued to walk, searching for an escape. He soon found a road that led to the countryside where once again he could disappear into a seemingly thin air.

As he trudged through the countryside, Jack became aware of a desperate thirst and the dry, sandy, gritty texture of his mouth. At that moment, he spotted an oasis in the desert, a farm with a water-well located about seventy feet away from a house. Jack mulled over the consequences of his actions. He had to consider the risks surrounding the satisfaction of his thirst, of getting a drink of water. What if he were seen? What would happen to him then? Would he be run off the property or would he be killed on the spot? His bodily need for water pushed the questions to the back of his mind and his feet toward the well. He scrutinized the house from a distance as he walked past. He didn't see anyone on the porch or in the yard. Jack cautiously approached the water-well that had a wooden bucket tied to a rope that could be cranked down into the well. Jack lowered the bucket, filled it with water and cranked it back up. He splashed the cool, wet well water all over his face, head and down his neck. He filled a big wooden spoon that was in the bucket with water several times and slurped about half a gallon of it before he quenched his thirst.

Jack heard the clip-clop sound of horse's hooves on the road and looked up to see a man on a wagon full of hay coming from the south. Jack rushed to make his way back to the road, hoping to hitch a ride. He held up his thumb to flag the driver. When the driver stopped, he asked Jack, "Where ya' headed?"

"I'm goin' bout eight miles from heah," said Jack.

The driver told Jack to hop on. The driver wasn't a man of much conversation; and he wasn't very interested in Jack, so he didn't ask any questions. That was the moment of peace that Jack needed.

Chapter 3

Uncle Lonnie, a tall thin man of olive complexion and receding hairline, lived with his wife Roxie on a hundred-acre cotton farm with two small grandchildren. Roxie, who was an excellent seamstress, had decorated their large seven room frame house with lovely furnishings and accessories. Uncle Lonnie was doing well for himself.

He was standing on the porch looking across the land when he saw the wagon draw near. Uncle Lonnie squinted to get a more focused look at the man who had hopped off the wagon and who was walking toward his property. Uncle Lonnie's heart leaped with surprise when he saw that it was his nephew Jack. He grabbed his nephew's hand, pulled him closer into a strong embrace and asked, "What you doing here? Come on in here and tell me what you doing here."

"Uncle Lonnie, I'm in trouble. I had a shootout wit the Sheriff. I shot him in his left arm, and a woman got shot in the crossfire. I thank she dead. Dat sheriff gonna strang me up if he catch me. I had tuh get outta Mississippi. I thought tuh ask ya if I could stay here wit you and Roxie for a spell, just until I can figga out my next steps."

Uncle Lonnie dropped his head and shook it from side to side. “Boy, you done went and got yourself in a fine mess, but you my brother’s son, you family. You can bunk down in the room next tuh where Roxie do her stitch'n.” Uncle Lonnie knew the Sheriff would search miles for Jack. He would search the entire South if he had to.

While continuing to keep a low profile, Jack spent the next days at his uncle’s place and helped around the farm. Uncle Lonnie had several farm-hands who had worked for him for many years. They had watched Jack grow up and knew about taking care of family. They tended to their own business; as a result, Jack did not worry about their turning him in.

Uncle Lonnie provided the sound advice to guide his nephew in the best direction for his life. Jack knew that he couldn’t stay anywhere in the South for too much longer.

Uncle Lonnie suggested, “When you get up North, use another name. You need tuh hide your identity. You can read and write. You'll be able tuh pass for one'a dem once you get out the South and always keep somethin' on yo noodle. Dhere’s plenty of work in the factories and steel mills up north. Go live wit the white folks. You be hard'da tuh find. Go tuh Chicago wit Paul and Mary. I'll get word tuh yo Mrs. I'll let everybody know dat you's here. I'll get Paul's whereabouts. You's make sure you get it from me, befo' you get a wiggle on.”

"I's gotta make it up north. If dat Sheriff catch me, he gonna strang me up."

"Just do what I say and everythang be okay."

When the newspapers came out around the town, Uncle Lonnie grabbed hold of any and all he could find. He combed through the pages to see if there were any stories about Jack. No, Jack wasn't in the newspapers, but handbills were distributed and "Wanted" posters were nailed to buildings all around town offering a reward for information on Jack's whereabouts.

After ten days, Jack left his uncle's with a small sack of personal items and money for food and lodging once he arrived in Chicago. It was enough for Jack to survive until he found employment.

Once again Jack had planned to stow away on the train, but when he got to the yard, he had to stay out of the light and out of the way of others in the yard. He hid in the dark spaces for what seemed like twenty minutes before he heard the sounds of the train rolling into the yard. Jack watched and waited for the Engineer to depart the train cab before he drew near. Jack knew Caruthersville was a rest stop and that the train would be there for a short spell.

Working quickly, he found an unlocked car and began to open the door where he found two hobos hiding among large sacks of rice. Jack hopped inside the car quickly and closed the door behind him. The other occupants didn't know quite what to make of Jack as he greeted them with a nod of his head and searched for a spot in the train car.

The three sat in silence sizing each other up for some minutes. In that time Jack saw that the hobos were Negros who seemed to be in their early thirties. One man was tall and slightly thin with a dirt smudge on his face and a torn shirt pocket. The other appeared to be around Jack's height but somewhat on the stocky side. He wore suspenders attached to his plaid pants and a cap. His clothes were rather dirty, all but his cap. Before long, the train jerked forward and proceeded to start its journey down the tracks.

After about thirty minutes of silence, Jack decided that he should say something.

"You's two heading tuh Chicago?"

The two men did not respond; they just looked at him. One man winked his eye while the other rummaged through his sack. The man who winked at Jack was wearing a flap-cap, the same type as Jack's, a golfer's cap. The hobo's cap caught Jack's interest, and he examined it more intently. He noticed the gray color with a firm rim and a fine line print running through it. Jack thought the cap looked pretty spiffy. As Jack admired the cap, the hobo looked strangely at him. The man didn't like the attention that Jack poured onto the cap, but they continued in silence. Eventually, exhaustion won over, and Jack knew he needed to sleep. He cushioned himself among the sacks of rice and fell into a deep, restful slumber.

Time seemed to whiz by and Jack awoke in what felt like a sauna with a parched throat and sweat drenched clothes. He knew the train had come to a stop, and he thirsted for water. Yet he was hesitant to pull out his canteen, for fear of having to share it with these men. Jack knew he didn't' have enough for three thirsty men, so he decided to conserve this water.

The train did not move for some time and Jack had to get off. He remembered the difficulty he had had before when he tried to open the train car door with the lock on the outside, but that would not be the case this time. The hobos were experts at extricating themselves from train cars with tools that somehow flipped the locking latch of the train. There they removed themselves and quickly departed company. In the open air, Jack saw that they weren't the only ones getting off the train. Others had also caught a free ride. Boxcars flew open and people jumped from the train. Jack had reached what he hoped to be his final destination.

Jack shielded his eyes against the bright sun shine and inhaled that city smell of the air filled with coal dust blowing out of the chimneys of the factories. From a distance, he detected the hustle and bustle of the people going about their daily routines. In Jack's immediate proximity, all he saw was dirt, grass, weeds and tracks, but he had made it to Chicago.

A big smile spread across Jack's face as a feeling of relief and safety came over his body. He found a secluded spot to relieve himself, and then walked along enjoying the city air, which was cooler and more refreshing compared with that in the boxcar. He rambled in his sack for his canteen and opened the container to gulp the coveted liquid down his throat like the thirsty man that he was.

Walking through the streets of Chicago, Jack thought about his reunion with his sister and brother. After finding a safe place to settle into, Jack would contact his siblings as soon as possible. Following Uncle Lonnie's instructions, he asked the first person he saw on the main street where he could find the Young Men's Christian Association.

Chapter 4

Jack took in the urban atmosphere of Chicago as he ventured from the train yard in the direction of the YMCA. Several clothing stores, a tailoring shop, a barber shop with a tall candy-cane striped pole and places to buy vittles sat nicely in a row under a large uniform curtain with large white stripes. Many people walked about and looked into the windows of the different establishments. No one hurried and no one noticed Jack. He felt his muscles release the tension as he relaxed and became lost in the crowd.

Now that he was in the North, Jack needed to test his ability to pass for white. Jack noticed a drug store with a sign with WHITE ONLY written in bold black letters. This was his opportunity to put his complexion to the test. He decided to go in. If he wasn't turned away immediately, he would know the results. He entered the store as if he belonged there and walked over to a board with ads posted. He spotted one that read, "Room at Boarding House, Must be quiet, Blower available," along with the address. Jack stared at the address for some time to commit it to memory. Afterwards he walked around the store to search for something to quench his thirst. When no one approached with angry, venomous demands to leave the store, Jack realized that he had passed the test. No one had recognized that Jack was a Negro.

With confidence he purchased a beverage and asked the man at the counter about the address of the boarding house. It was almost a mile away.

Leaving the drug store, Jack continued in the direction of the YMCA. He was hoping to get something to eat at the YMCA, to clean himself up, and to rest for the evening. Jack also knew that he needed to pretend to be younger than he was. After all, The YMCA was for young men. Jack was a grown man. Fortunately, he looked younger than he actually was, and at this moment, he was thankful for his youthful looks. He hoped that he would be able to convince others. At that point, Jack remembered what his uncle said, “You'll need tuh change yo name.”

Jack arrived at a stop for the double decker motor bus where several people waited to board. All but one were white folks. Jack politely tipped his hat to all and stood at the back of the crowd. When the bus arrived, everyone, except the Negro lady, got on. The Negro lady, who was the last to board, paid her five cents and proceeded to the top level of the bus. Jack, still testing whether or not he could pass for white, sat on the lower level in the front of the motor bus. When no one said anything to Jack, he rode quietly until the bus reached his destination.

A blind man with a walking stick, an older gentleman with white whiskers and a round face, rode the motor bus with the other passengers. The man had on cheaters. Jack wondered why in the world a blind person would need cheaters. Jack had seen blind people wearing dark glasses before but never cheaters. He looked at the man's overall appearance – a Santa Claus without the red suit.

The double decker bus held about forty people. It appeared to be full to capacity Out of all the folks on the bus, only one person paid attention to Jack, an older woman, who took the bold liberty to wink at him. Jack felt uncomfortable with the unwanted attention coming from one of his elders. He quickly repositioned his gaze to the sights from the windows as the bus rolled through the streets.

Jack rode the rest of the way with his elbow on the ledge of the opened window and stared out. The bus felt a little cold, but it was better than walking. Jack was in Chicago, passing for white and riding a motor bus. He was alive and life was going in a new direction.

Upon entering the YMCA, several young men, ranging from the age of thirteen to eighteen, mingled around. Seeing them, Jack was sure he could pass for eighteen. The gentleman at the desk was a man who looked to be in his thirties. Jack introduced himself.

"How you do Suh? My name is *Wade Johnson*. I's wondering, if you might have a cot available for the night?"

The gentleman introduced himself, "Hello, Mr. Johnson, you can call me John. You need a cot for the night?"

"I's just got in town from Georgia. Been traveling for two days now and in need of a good night's rest. I's hoping dis here Christian Association might be able tuh rest me for the night. I'll be gone first thang in the morning."

"*Wade*, we are currently serving lunch and you are welcome to eat. Supper will be served at six. Let me show you where you can bathe and rest for the night."

The sleeping cots, about a hundred, were located in a large room. The bathing facilities, with large metal tubs filled with fresh water several times daily, were located on an upper level. John could smell that Jack needed grooming and provided him with a piece of soap and a drying cloth.

With a hot bath and a good dinner meal, Jack rested well through the night. He awoke early the next morning, freshened up and proceeded to breakfast. He ran into John who informed him about the free clothing available to residents. After breakfast Jack found the clothing, selected a few pieces and neatly placed them in his sack. Later Jack left the YMCA to search for the address of the boarding house that he had stored in his memory from the drug store.

Chapter 5

Jack had been in Chicago for almost twenty-four hours when he arrived at the boarding house located around the Irish Parish that attended St James Church on 29th and Wabash.

Jack knocked on the door of the boarding house, a cobblestone structure with a sitting porch. An older white woman, a petite, frail looking brunette with a hint of gray in her hair, came to the door. She glared at him over the rim of her cheater, as Jack proceeded to tell the woman why he was there.

“Hello Ma’am, My name is Wade Johnson. I’m here about the room in the ad I read at the drug store.”

The woman responded, “Yes, young man, I did place an ad in the drug store. My name is Mrs. Smith. Please come in and follow me; I’ll show you the room.” Mrs. Smith hadn't blinked an eye. She just knew Jack was a white man. His confidence swelled within, walking behind Mrs. Smith; he had succeeded in passing for white for the third time since he’d arrived in Chicago. Jack saw that he wasn’t going to have any problem with his new identity now that he was up north.

Jack inspected the room. It was a small room with a small chest that had a pitcher and wash basin on top. A cot sat against the wall. Jack sensed that this would be the perfect place to stay. Coming from a family of eleven children, he was not use to having a lot of space to himself. He turned to Mrs. Smith to ask about the cost and the date when payment was due. When she replied, Jack said, "I'll take it, if you'll have me, Ma'am. Your ad said, 'must be quiet.' You won't even know I'm here."

"Okay then. You seem like a fine young man. Where did you say you're from?"

"I's from Georgia. Been traveling for two days," Jack said with a swift tongue and a charming smile, one that drove the ladies crazy back home.

"Oh, ummm, I don't mean tuh pry Ma'am, but is dhere a Mis'ta Smith?

"Well, there was, I'm sorry to say that Mr. Smith passed away a few years ago. His name was Clyde. I sure do miss my Clyde."

"Let me 'spress my symp'thy, Ma'am." With that, Jack paid Mrs. Smith two weeks' rent and turned back to go to his room.

Following Jack with her gaze, Mrs. Smith spotted the small sack containing Jack's personal belongings. "Is that all you have with you?" she asked.

"I have a few mo thangs; I will tote dem later."

Taking a rest for a couple of days, Jack settled into the room and made it his new home. He knew he had to find a place to work, to get some changes of clothes, and to buy personal products; the money that Uncle Lonnie had given him would not last forever. Mrs. Smith supplied him with information about the needed resources that Jack could find in the neighborhood. He discovered a second hand store and purchased a medium suitcase for a little of nothing. He also picked up a few items for his personal hygiene and found a place where he could obtain free clothing. Jack placed all his items into the used suitcase. Not wanting to draw any suspicion from Mrs. Smith or any of the boarders, Jack thought his appearance would be more believable if he were able to stick to his new story, toting a used case with a few scars instead of a new one.

Jack was very careful with whom he spoke. He had to start a new life and make new connections, but he didn't want to do this too quickly. Jack searched any and all of the newspapers he could to see if any news about him and the shooting in Mississippi had traveled north. To his relief, he had found nothing about the incident.

Jack felt the need to contact Lonnie to let his uncle know that he had made it up North and that he was okay. He thought about sending a telegram and chanced writing two letters in hope that his family would receive them. He knew that his uncle would contact his Papa, who, in turn, would contact Jack's wife Bessie and his siblings. He wanted to let those close to him know of his new identity as Wade Johnson and his new residence in Chicago. Jack anxiously waited to hear from them.

A few days later, Jack found employment performing various duties as a gopher at one of the many steel mills in and around the city. This job was exactly what Jack needed to cover his tracks because he could be any place, at any time, running any number of errands as part of his job responsibilities. No one would question his absence.

The days turned into weeks and Jack continued to stay to himself. He frequented the neighborhood diner *Ethel's Place,* a quaint little restaurant that was strictly for white folks and that was only crowded on Sundays. Red, round tables with two matching red chairs filled the center of the diner. Booths dressed with table cloths ran along the side walls. Jack became one of the regulars, always sitting at a booth or a table facing the door to see all who entered the diner, just in case he felt the need to make a quick exit.

Chapter 6

After five weeks in Chicago, Jack became comfortable with his surroundings. The neighborhood stayed clean and quiet. He quickly learned the public transportation system and moved about the city easily. Most of all, he was passing as *one of them* which afforded him all the advantages of the privileged race. Yes, Jack felt as though things were going well.

He went for a walk some evenings to think about his next move, but all too often those thoughts turned into memories of his family: his brother Paul, whose birth name was Lanier, had moved to Chicago many years prior looking for work. Jack thought about Mississippi and his family often. He had a strong inkling to see his wife (Bessie) with another one due any day and his boys, two-year old twins. During her first pregnancy with the twins, Bessie craved the chalky taste of the clay dirt and had to have it at least once a month. And just as she had craved the clay, Jack craved the hooch, the moonshine he had tasted back home, which ran plentiful in Chicago, thanks to *Al Capone* and his bootlegging gangsters.

Jack was sitting on the porch when he heard the blower sound from within the house. Three weeks had passed since he had sent the letters to his family members. The blower sounded again and Mrs. Smith answered.

"Hello. Yes there's a Wade Johnson here. Hold for a moment. I will get him."

When Jack heard the voice, he recognized the deep baritone was that of his brother Paul. Although Jack was anxious to talk with his brother at that moment, he knew that the ears of others would open wide to learn who was calling the boarder that basically kept to himself. So he kept the conversation short and gave Paul the address to Ethel's Place with the instructions to meet him there on Sunday. Paul often forgot that Jack's real name was Eugene and now he would need to remember to call him *Wade*.

***

Paul, a tall, thin man with dark hair, arrived at the diner Sunday, as planned. He too had been able to pass. He was in his mid-thirties and walked with a limp. Almost every table and chair in Ethel's was occupied, but Paul spotted his youngest brother sitting close to the entrance of the diner. Jack stood to embrace his brother, elated; and Paul, in high spirits, returned the affection with strong arms and a wide grin.

Jack asked question after question, not giving Paul a chance to answer: "How you doing? How's Mary? Where you's stay? Do you's stay far from here? "You talked tuh Papa? What he say? Dey still looking for me?" When Jack stopped to take a breath, Paul took his turn to answer as much as he could.

"I don't live too far from here, but you do bess taking the streetcar. Mary doing fine. She live on 39th Street. She got the sniffles and it's damp outside today, so she decided not tuh come. She sends her love."

Jack told Paul to contact his wife. "I know she worried. Let her know dat you saw me and dat I'm doing okay. Tell her dat I really miss her and the young'uns. Let her know dat I don't want her tuh try and contact me. I'll send for dem when the time is right."

They continued with their conversation after the waitress took their order. Paul took the time to take a good look at Jack as the lad resumed with his inquiries. He was the same old Jack, Paul's baby brother, always getting into trouble.

People continued entering the diner. The waitresses had their hands full with all the Sunday business. All of a sudden, a loud crashing sound rang throughout the entire establishment. Jack, still a little edgy dipped down into the seat. The sound of the metal bowl hitting the restaurant's wooden floor startled all the occupants, but Jack had a flashback of the shootout. Regaining his composure and not wanting to attract too much attention,

Jack sat back in his seat and focused more on Paul, who had started to talk again.

“Papa told me tuh tell you tuh stay put. Dey's still looking for you. Dey's searching for you all over Mississippi. Bessie and the twins doing fine. Papa and Baby Girl been helping Bessie wit the twins, so don't worry bout dem none. Yo wife a little upset bout you. She wanna come see you. Now tell me what happen? What caused you tuh have a shootout wit the Sheriff. Which sheriff was it?”

“It was dat Sheriff Rogers. He don't care much for me no how. Dem white women be looking at me all full a lust and wantin’ and dis be getting him upset. He be going around selling hooch. I thank he drank more hooch dan he sell. Anyway, we’s havin' a fish-fry at the Rosebank Methodist Baptist Church in Coila after service. Everybody having a good time. Old man Percy Jones was playing his guitar. I wanted tuh see him do his little dance and play the guitar at the same time. I was playing around and shot off my pistol. Well, dat Sheriff come by. He always comin’ by the church after service. Anyway, he com' a spatting at me. He said somebody tol’ him, I shot off my pistol. He told me dat he knew I had a pistol and dat I bess turn it over. I told him I what'n turning nothin' over tuh him, so he pulled his pistol on me. The next thang I know, we's squirting bullets. Folks had tuh run for cover inside the church. I hit him in the left arm, but Alma Lark got killed in the crossfire. He shot dat woman; he was the one shooting in that direction. I was standing wit my back tuh the church. My bullets was going out on the road. I had tuh get the hell outta dhere. I hated leaving Bessie and the young'uns like dat, but I had tuh go. I knew if dat sheriff got hold'a me, he was gonna strang me up. I knew he was gonna try and get the goods on me and blame me for Alma's death. You know a black man's word cain't go up gainst no white man, not in Mississippi."

The waitress returned with their plates of food, steaming, smothered chicken and onions and rice and gravy, looking and smelling saintly. Jack started to eat as soon as his plate was set on the table. He always wolfed his food down when he was excited; he had been doing this since he was a kid. Paul told him to slow down so that Jack would be able to at least taste his food. Then, Paul started to speak again: "You keep laying-low. Dat Sheriff done took thangs long past Mississippi. He done got the G-men involved in dis case. Dat bullet you put in his left arm caused him tuh lose his arm. He ain't too happy bout it neither. He out for blood. Papa ain't too happy bout it neither. He worried sick bout you. Papa getting old. He done had tuh deal wit many beefs cause'a us. "

Jack furrowed his eyebrows with concern about the burden he had brought on his father. Hoping to lighten his mood and to give Paul something good to report to their father, Jack stated, "Tell Papa everythang going to be okay. I was able get on at one of the steel mills. I just been going tuh work and keeping tuh myself. I got a package dat I need you tuh send home."

Jack looked around the restaurant for prying eyes; and, seeing none, he discreetly handed a sealed envelope to his brother, which Paul slipped inside his jacket pocket. He then went on to tell Jack some places that he might want to visit in Chicago -- after things cooled off -- and some places to avoid. They finished their meals and departed with another exchange of brotherhood. Paul called after Jack as he walked away, "Come by my place one Sunday af'ta Church; take care'a yo self."

Paul sent Jack's package to their sister in Mississippi, the one whom they called Baby Girl. She was just that, the last of eleven children. Her birth name was Lucinda, and she and Jack were about five years apart in age. She would give the package to Bessie.

***

Later, sitting in his room at the boarding house, Jack reflected on the shoot-out with the Sheriff. He thought about Alma Lark, an upstanding member of the church. Jack knew that sooner or later, he would pay for this crime. He also knew the Sheriff would never confess to the fact that his bullets were the only ones being fired in Alma's direction. Jack also understood that the shootout wasn't the real reason that the Sheriff was after him. "Dat Sheriff don't care nothing about no Negroes being killed. He just got a bellyache 'bout his arm. Dat Sheriff Rogers always starting beefs. He be selling dat hooch; he an' other folks be gettin' drunk, and playing craps; den fights be breaking out." Jack wished he had shot both his arms off.

Chapter 7

Now back at Jennie's house in Mississippi, her husband Wilbert was off the chain-gang and back with his wife and children. He wasn't a very pleasant man; as a matter of fact, his personality down-right nasty and mean spirited. He had an evil heart to go along with the pistol that he kept on him at all times.

Jennie often wondered what had attracted her to Wilbert in the first place. She supposed that it was the way he carried himself with his nice, neat clothing, like a solider in uniform. He was slightly tall around five feet ten inches with a sexy attractiveness that had pulled Jennie into him, as a magnet attracts metal. Now that Wilbert had been home for ten weeks, Jennie fretted over her pregnancy. She was fifteen weeks heavy with Jack's child. No explanation would pacify Wilbert's reaction. And then to make matters worse, Jack's wife Bessie had just given birth to Earl. Bessie and Jack now had three young'uns.

Moreover, Sheriff Rogers carried on his search for Jack with a vengeance. He was out to find the man, a colored, who has cost him an arm. When the local authorities couldn't find his enemy in Mississippi, the Sheriff and his Klan took matters into their own hands. Hoping that John Brewer was somewhere drunk. -- Papa Brewer, quite the ladies' man, was known for drinking until he passed out -- they burst rudely into the Brewer household and dragged Jack's two brothers, James and Norman, out of their beds at gunpoint. Jack's stepmother Bertha stood at the door, fretting as she watched the Sheriff and his Klan haul her sons off into the dark whisper of the rainy night. She prayed intensely that they would return breathing and intact with all their bodily parts. She wept, praying that Lord Jesus would watch over her sons. One of the last sounds James and Norman heard was their mother's powerful prayer, and they hoped that her prayers would be answered.

Sheriff Rogers and his Klan took the Brewer brothers deep into the dense, dark woods where the wind whistled eerily through the trees. The Sheriff wanted to keep this a private matter. No one would witness his act of vengeful torture of the brothers, except the ones who inflicted the punishment.

Forcing the brothers to their knees, the Klan surrounded them and pointed shotguns and pistols at their heads and bodies. The sheriff spat out questions with venomous shouts: "Where the hell is he? We know you two heathens know where he is. You better tell us."

James yelled in an insolent voice, "We don't know where he is! We ain't seen him!"

His stepbrother Norman followed with more fear than defiance,

"We swear! We don't know!"

"You can just say goodbye tuh yo brother, because when I find him, I'm gonna strang him up by his neck, and dats a promise. I'd outta blow yo heads off right now."

The Sheriff and his Klan persisted with the sadistic threats to end the lives of James and Norman, but Rogers knew better than to cause any physical harm to the brothers. These Negroes were an external phenomenon of John Brewer's lineage with strong familial ties to Mississippi's Ex-Governor Earl Leroy Brewer. *Blood Is Thicker Than Color.*

Chapter 8

Several weeks had passed since Jack arrived in Chicago and he had been laying-low: going to work and then back to the boarding house and frequenting Ethel's' on Sundays. Sometimes, Jack sat on the long porch of the boarding house to enjoy the night breezes of summer, but he hadn't really spoken with anyone in great detail, even the people he commuted with day-in and day-out. He decided that he would venture out to visit Paul.

When Jack reached the address that Paul had given him, he arrived at a large brownstone housing unit. He remembered that Paul stayed in the rear of the housing unit. He proceeded to the back of the complex, where he found several doors. Jack knocked on the door of the unit that was closest to the alley on the first level. His brother hearing the knock responded with "Who calling?". After realizing it was Jack, he swung his door wide open to welcome him.

"Jack, how are you? Its good tuh see you; come on in. I'm trying fix somethin' tuh eat. Can you stay for supper? Nothin' like a home cooked meal. Dis place ain't much size, but I'm doing okay. I'm saving up for a bigger place. Come on over here and sit a spell. It'll be a while befo' supper ready, making bean soup."

Jack looked around his brother's place. Paul's home was a cozy, modern day unit with all the amenities and grooming facilities. A pair of wall lanterns and a kerosene lamp sitting on the table provided plenty of light. Two chairs set on opposite sides of the table. Wide striped wallpaper covered the walls. Against one wall was Paul's bed across from the table. It was truly a man's palace.

Waiting for the soup to finish cooking, the two men talked. Jack wanted to send for his wife Bessie to come for a visit. He told Paul that he really wanted to see his family, especially the new baby.

Paul stated, "Maybe Bessie and Baby Girl can come together. Dhere's still plenty of folks at the house tuh watch the twins for a few days."

"Dey growing-up so fast on me," Jack remembered. "Dey the spittin' image of Bessie. Maybe she and the new baby and Baby Girl, maybe dey can come for Labor Day. Nobody even notice dey gone, especially if the twins stay dhere. I know Bessie done had the baby. I gots tuh see the baby."

Paul told Jack that he would get word to their papa. He was sure that Papa Brewer wouldn't have any problem helping with the trip. "But we got to be real careful 'bout the plans," said Jack, "cause I'm sure dat Sheriff got his ears and nose all around town."

Chapter 9

Next morning came and Jack, as usual, prepared for work, humming a little tune. He was in a good mood, thinking of the plan that he and Paul talked about the previous night, envisioning his wife Bessie enfolded in his longing arms.

Jack entered the mill still humming as he walked past one of his co-worker, giving him the courtesy of a greeting as he passed. Although he tended to stay to himself, he managed to get along well with his co-workers and bosses. Jack's good mood was noticeable to his co-worker who asked, "What you so happy about this morning?"

"Oh, it's just a great day. The sun is shining and life is good."

"Don't nothing make a man smile like that but a broad."

Jack just laughed and commenced his day's work. Jack worked hard that week and looked forward to the weekend. He thought about buying a new suit; he wanted to look his best for Bessie while she was in Chicago.

The warm weather was on its way out. The days had become overcast and fall appeared to be slipping in quickly. When the weekend came, Jack decided to make a trip to Maxwell Street, starting out early and stopping first at Ethel's Place for a breakfast. Afterwards, he hopped a trolley car to Maxwell Street. He had heard that the clothing stores on Maxwell had the finest men's suits that could be custom tailored to fit.

In 1926 the Maxwell shopping district ran from Halsted Street just south of Roosevelt Road to 16th Street with retail businesses, Chicago blues, open flea markets and polish sausages lining the streets. Maxwell Street Market consumers were predominantly Negroes and the business owners were predominately Jews. With a long standing history in Chicago, the Maxwell Street consumers had changed over the years with the Coloreds coming in during the Great Migration.

Jack was a little taken by all the commotion, but he quickly learned that there were deals to be made when it came to purchasing things on Maxwell. With his smooth talk, Jack did well on Maxwell that day.

Hearing about the Chicago Winters, Jack knew that his lightweight jacket would never do. So, he bought an overcoat and some footgear, along with a suit that he had tailored to fit. He thought to surprise Bessie with something special. He found an exquisite multicolored scarf with a beautiful butterfly design and added it to his purchases.

Leaving Maxwell, Jack headed for his sister's place with his packages in tow. Paul had given him Mary's address the night before. Jack was excited about seeing the rest of his family, whom he had not seen since his niece was a baby and he was a youngster. After thirty minutes on the motor bus, he arrived a few blocks from the four-unit gray stone where Mary lived in a first-floor apartment with her husband and daughter.

Jack quickened his steps to Mary's front door and knocked. A few seconds later Mary opened the door as wide as she opened her arms and her smile answering, "Jack, come on in. Its good tuh see you. Give me a big hug. You's been shopping? Look like Christmas came early. You been over on Maxwell Street?"

"I sure have. Its good tuh see yuh Mary. Sorry, it took me so long tuh come by. I's just been going tuh work and laying-low."

"I heard what happen back home. You keep laying-low. You looking mighty fine. Put yo thangs over dhere in the corner. Jake and Ella in the back room. I was just fixing somethin' tuh eat. Come on in the back."

The apartment contained a large front room, one nice size sleeping room, a small cooking space with a large open eating area. A long hallway with a bathroom ran inside the space, connecting it nicely. Mary's creative decorating skills presented a real hominess to the place.

Mary, thin and tall with high cheek bones, was the second oldest child in the family and slightly older than Paul. She had long, fine, dark brown hair and fair colored skin just like Jack. She favored their mama so much, Jack thought, her mannerisms from the way she held her cigarette to the way she hiccupped a little bit at the end of her laughter reminded him so much of their mother.

Their mother didn't live long after Baby Girl was born, and their Papa remarried. Mary didn't get along with her stepmother Bertha and with the difficulties of life in the South for people of color, Mary moved to Chicago, returned to the South only two other times for a visit and then stopped altogether. However, Mary made sure to stay in contact with Papa John Brewer, who always shared her letters with the family.

Mary's husband, Jake, a tall man of around six feet five inches with brown skin, wasn't very educated, but he had a great sense of humor and lovingly adored her with all his heart.

Jake and Mary's fourteen year old daughter, Ella, was the typical city teenager. She had a gorgeous cinnamon complexion, a beautiful smile and a laugh that brought about giggles from anyone who heard it. Ella didn't know much about the South, only what she had heard from her parents and that was nothing good

-- nothing good in the South for colored folks. She also heard that she would never go.

Ella looked up from a book that she was reading and said with a smile, “Hey, so you my Uncle Jack?”

Jack responded, “Hey there, young lady. You all grown-up. How old you now?”

“I'm fourteen.”

“And you’s a little dish.” Ella just giggled and blushed as she quickly went back to reading her book.

Taking in all the love of family and home, Jack saw his brother-in-law who stood to greet him with a full smile and a hearty handshake. Jake asked, “Is dis little Jack? I heard you was in town. Man, you ain’t little no mo. Set on down and take a load off.”

Jack replied with a short laugh, “Yep, I picked up some thangs over on Maxwell Street. I wanted tuh buy myself a suit and an overcoat for the cold weather. Just last night, I had a spill wit Paul bout bringing Bessie and the new baby here for a visit. We thought the holidays might be a good time for the three of ‘em tuh visit. Baby Girl could come wit ‘em. Dhere's still plenty folks back home tuh see after the twins. Plus, I wanna see the baby. I know he look like me. I just know he do, because the twins look like Bessie. Dis number three for us and he just gotta look like me."

Mary chimed in, "Bringing Bessie, the baby, and Baby Girl for the holiday sound mighty fine. We can get together over here. Paul can come over too. It be nice tuh get the family together. It's been a long time since I been around family."

Jack responded, "Yep, it would be nice tuh get together. I need tuh get out mo. I just been staying at the boarding house, eatin' at the neighborhood diner, goin' tuh work at the steel mills, and jus' staying tuh myself. I wanted -- *I needed* -- tuh stop by tuh see my family and say somethin' tuh y'all."

Feeling the loneliness pouring out of Jack and wanting to make him feel at home, Jake asked, "Well, you staying for supper, ain't you? You mo dan welcome."

"Not today, but thank yuh. I wanna get back tuh my room and rest a spell. I been putting in a lot'a time at the Mill, but I'll see y'all on the holiday."

Jake responded, "How bout'a roasted pig?"

"Dat sound like some mighty fine eating. I b'lieve I will join y'all.

My room at the boarding house will be waitin' for me whenever I get dhere" Jack answered with a smile on his face.

Chapter 10

It was the Friday before Labor Day. Bessie, Baby Girl and the new baby Earl were due to arrive by train on the next day. Jack planned to meet them at Union Station. It had been seven months, since he had seen his sister and his wife who was five months pregnant at the time. He was feeling, at the same time, glad and nervous with the anticipation of seeing his family, so much so that he struggled to sleep, tossing and turning all night long.

Unable to sleep, Jack got up early Saturday morning washed and dressed for the day. He stopped on his way to breakfast at the diner to purchase his usual newspaper. Around seven a.m., Jack entered the diner and sat at his favorite booth facing the door. He scanned the diner, which was somewhat quiet, and observed the usual morning crowd. Soon after he adapted to the atmosphere, Jack gave his order to the waitress who always took his order.

"Morning, Mr. Johnson, What's your pleasure?"
"I'll be having my lucky breakfast dis morning," Jack replied with a smile.

As she wrote the order on his receipt, the waitress repeated the details, "That's three eggs, sunny-side up, grits, ham, biscuits and a glass of buttermilk."

"Yes, Ma'am!"

"One lucky breakfast coming right up." With that, the waitress turned on her heels and left to place the order with the cook. She returned a few minutes later with a glass of cold buttermilk. Jack thanked her and opened his newspaper. He searched page by page, looking for any mention of his name until the smells of his deliciously hot breakfast distracted his attention. The waitress placed his lucky breakfast on the table in front of him, while Jack folded his newspaper to put away temporarily. Besides he didn't see anything about himself in the paper. After finishing his meal, Jack returned to the newspaper scrutinizing the articles in his search for anything about him.

After breakfast, Jack headed north, straight for Union Station, which took about forty minutes. At approximately nine o'clock he entered the station and walked into the Great Hall. Looking up, Jack stared with amazement at the colossal Corinthian columns standing at least 100 feet high and serving as structural supports of the Great Hall, which was crowned with a vaulted skylight. The natural light bounced off sparkling marble walls and floors where polished wooden benches sat sparsely in the wide open space. Coming back down to ground level, Jack felt a little hesitant about whether he should stand or sit and whether he should merge with the crowd or stand off by himself. If he merged with the crowd, someone might recognize him. If he stood alone, he might stand out and move even more in the spotlight of recognition. He chose to merge with the crowd and took a seat on one of the benches to wait for the train to arrive. He focused his attention on the marble pillars and daydreamed about his life and family back in Mississippi. Jack pictured his Papa working on the farm and saw himself feeding the cattle, picking cotton, pulling ears off the tall green stalks of corn. He thought that he would never be able to do that again, unless he got caught and ended up on the prison farm. He hoped to return to Mississippi one day, but not as part of a chain-gang.

Swarms of people shuffled into and out of the station, arriving and departing for the Labor Day holiday. According to bits and pieces of conversation floating through the air, Jack learned that the train coming from Mississippi was always late, so Jack made himself as comfortable as he could, took out his morning paper and turned to the comic section.

Finally, the voice over the loudspeaker announced the arrival of the City of New Orleans on Track 8 and Jack folded his paper, tucked it under his arm and moved quickly toward the gate for Track 8. This New Orleans train was also the train from Mississippi. People unloaded in droves and enveloped Jack in a wave of bodies that he attempted to move against. It took him a good twenty minutes to spot Baby Girl, Bessie, and his new baby boy Earl. He raised his arms, attempting to flag their attention as he headed in their direction. His sister, Baby Girl, was the first to spot Jack and turned to Bessie, "Dhere's Jack!". Baby Girl waved back excitedly and threw him a big smile. Jack seemed to float in a cloud of euphoria as he made his way over to his loved ones. Bessie, too, seem to hover above ground when she saw her handsome husband coming toward her.

Bessie was a caramel colored woman sprinkled with freckles. She had already possessed a large bosom on her medium frame, but now it was even larger, since she was breastfeeding. Her hair was much thicker than Jack's, but it had softness that he loved to feel against his skin. Bessie was the love of Jack's life.

"Y'all made it! How was the trip?" asked Jack breathing a sigh of relief. He embraced all three into his big, loving arms, giving everyone a welcoming kiss on the cheek. He returned to Bessie's wanting lips and pressed his own lips gently against her soft flesh, allowing his loving desires to ooze and mingle with hers.

A cooing sound coming from between them brought Jack and Bessie back down to earth, to the train platform on Track 8. When they parted slightly, Jack saw his new baby boy for the first time. Jack fixed his gaze on his youngest son all bundled in blue, who was a little more than three months old and -- just like the twins -- he favored Bessie.

Bessie responded, “Everythang was good. It was kind'a hard leaving the twins, but I did need a break. After you left so suddenly, I had tuh change a few thangs around, but Baby Girl been helping me out and Papa Brewer been giving me some money tuh keep up wit the bills and take care of the young‘uns. He just worried ‘bout you. Oh yeah, befo’ I forget, I did get yo package from Paul. The boys really do miss dey daddy. I know dey just some young'uns, but dey know you ain't been dhere. You missed dey second birthday. I missed you too,” she said so softly that he had to pull her closer to him to hear her voice.

Jack grabbed the luggage and led his family toward the station. Once outside, Jack pointed to a tall man dressed nicely in a suit and driver’s cap, standing next to a European luxury car. Baby Girl recognized her brother immediately and ran to greet him, almost jumping into his opened arms. Bessie took in the view with a full, opened mouth and wide-eyed surprise.

Baby Girl shouted, “Paul, is dat you? Why, I cain’t believe my eyes. Just look at you and look at what you done done for yo’sef wit dis fine boiler.” Bessie stepped away from Jack momentarily to receive Paul’s welcome and to admire the 1925 Mercedes-Benz. Paul worked as a chauffeur for a wealthy family who lived on Prairie Avenue and with whom he had developed a most trusting relationship. So, when Jack approached Paul with his plan to meet Baby Girl, Bessie, and his new son at the train station, all Paul had to do was to ask his employer, and Jack's wish was granted. He wanted his Bessie to feel like a queen.

Baby Girl squealed with excitement, "Ooooh, Paul! Is dis yo boiler?"

Paul smiled at his sister's childlike enthusiasm and replied, "Nope, Baby Girl, Dis not mine, It belong tuh the man I work for, but he was kind'a enough tuh let me use it for today."

With that, he opened the passenger front door and offered his hand to Baby Girl to help his sister adjust herself into the luxurious leather seat. He then moved swiftly to the rear passenger side to open the door for Bessie and Baby Earl. Jack was standing close by, so Bessie passed the baby to Jack to hold while Paul offered his hand to help her into the roomy rear soft – as -- butter leather seat. Once she was all adjusted, Bessie reached for Baby Earl and Jack set the baby gently into her waiting arms. Jack then moved to the rear of the car to help Paul organize the luggage into the rear of the vehicle, making sure not to touch the sides of the car for fear of scratches and dents.

After securing the luggage, Jack moved to the driver's side rear door and climbed in with the agility of an acrobat on a trapeze.

Paul took his place in the driver's seat, and started the Benz. Glancing at his passengers and making sure that all were comfortable, Paul checked his mirrors and eased the car smoothly into the traffic. The car seemed to glide over the city streets as Paul proceeded toward Mary's home.

The smile on her face and in her eyes signaled to Paul that Bessie was still in awe at the mode of transportation moving them effortlessly through the lanes, avenues and boulevards of Chicago. After taking in some of the sights along the way, she chimed in, "Paul, dis Boiler sho is nice."

Paul asked, "How's thangs back home?"

"I'll tell y'all all about it when we get tuh Mary's but thangs not going so good wit dat Sheriff. Papa hanging in dhere cause he hard-boiled, Baby Girl stated. "We had some trouble, but you know Papa; he don't let nothin' get him down. He missing everybody though and he send his love."

Twenty-five minutes later Paul parked the luxury auto in front of Mary's to find her sitting in the window eagerly awaiting their arrival. She called excitedly to her husband and daughter, "Dey's here," and ran to open the front door. Jake and Ella proceeded to the front of the apartment. Mary and Baby Girl -- rushed toward each other, enfolding themselves in a hug. Jack quickly introduced Bessie to the rest of the family. "Dis here is my wife

Bessie." Jake and Ella said hello in unison. Mary had finished embracing Baby Girl and gave Bessie a hug too. Jack took this opportunity to cradle Baby Earl and examine every part of his little body, looking for any mark of resemblance to himself or his family.

Mary introduced Baby Girl to her husband and her daughter. "Jake, Ella dis my Baby Sister Lucinda, but we's call her *Baby Girl.*"

Y'all come on in and make yo'selves right at home; rest yo'selves. I know you may be tired after that long train ride," Jake responded.

Ella said "Hi" with a shy smile and a giggle to all. Mary's words spilled out several sentences all in one breath: "Y'all hungry? How's thangs back home?" She walked toward Jack and reached for the baby. "Let me see dat baby. Ooooh, wheee! He look just like his mama.."

Jack stood at her side with a discerning look on his face, his mind racing with thoughts. Mary and Paul knew Bessie's family, but Bessie was a young'un the last time they had encountered her.

Looking at Mary as if to study her, Baby Girl thought she was the spitting image of their mama based on a photo back home. Baby girl didn't actually have living memories of their mama who died shortly after Baby Girl was born.

Baby Girl was eighteen years old and quite mature, the type of maturity that comes from being the youngest of eleven children. She stood at approximately five feet, four inches and possessed a gorgeous figure. Jack was just a few inches taller. Baby Girl was considered to be a beautiful woman and shared the fair skin tone that her siblings had. Her hair was a medium length that fell to her shoulders in a combination of waves and curls.

Back home, Baby Girl worked around the farm but with Jack gone, she tried to provide the much needed additional help that Papa needed. Learning that she would accompany Bessie and Baby Earl to Chicago made her almost giddy with relief, relieved that she would be getting away from the anxiety and stress she experienced at home. Jack's sudden getaway from a sheriff who was seeking revenge took a heavy toll on the whole family. Plus she missed her brother and looked forward to seeing him, as well as Paul and Mary. It had been too long.

Mary and Jake lived in a one-bedroom apartment. Their daughter Ella slept in a swing-down bed that was hidden behind a large door located in the front room. To accommodate her sister's needs, Mary had placed a cot against the wall in the room where they ate their meals, so Baby Girl would have a place to sleep.

Bessie, Jack and the baby would stay at the Southmoor Hotel on 47th Street and South Parkway.

After everyone seemed to settle into their seats at the table, Mary went promptly to the stove and started dishing up the vittles. Baby Girl had looked forward to getting to know her niece and started talking with Ella. Jake moved the rocking chair from the enclosed back porch for Bessie so she could sit comfortably with Baby Earl. Before the arrival of their family members, Jake and Mary had discussed how nice it would be to give Bessie and Jack's baby a gift to welcome him into the world. Jake was a most excellent carpenter possessing the skills of a master craftsman. With his expertise, he fashioned out of a large block of wood a bassinet engraved with curling vines and exotic leaves just for the baby. Mary filled the bottom of the bassinet and lined the sides with smooth padding, which she covered with soft yellow cotton fabric. When Bessie saw the bassinet, her eyes filled with tears of gratitude. She looked up at Jake who was a watery vision before her and thanked him and Mary for such a thoughtful present. He placed Earl tenderly onto the softly covered padding in the bassinet. Jack stood to take Jake's hand in his own two hands and showed his admiration and appreciation with a firm grasp and shake. Then they all deposited themselves around the large table for eight, it was then that Jack noticed the same scroll of vines and exotic leaves on the trim of the dining table and chair backs that appeared on the bassinet. Jack looked back at Jake and said, "You sho can carve up some wood."

They sat at the table eating the scrumptious dinner that Mary had prepared: collard greens, potato salad with pimentos, fried chicken, and corn bread. Jack sat directly across the table from Bessie to admire her beauty. Bessie had just breastfed their baby, and Jack ached with passion for his wife. He sat there undressing Bessie with his eyes, as he dreamed about caressing her soft body and running his tongue all over her luscious breast.

After dinner Baby Girl changed Jack's mood quickly when she began to tell the others what happened in Mississippi and what the Sheriff and his Klan had done to James and Norman.

"Dat Sheriff and his Klan come'a busting in during the night, while Papa wuh'nt even home -- I don't know where Papa was -- and dey took James and Norman out in the woods over dhere by the old creek. Y'all know the place, it's close by but full'a woods. Don't nobody ever go out dhere. Anyway, dey had dem rifles and rope like dey was gonna strang'um up. Dey wouldn't a come in dhere like dat, if Papa had'a been home. Mama Bertha stood at the door weeping. I just started howlin' like an old rooster. Norman told us that dey threatened tuh kill'em, but dey just kept'em deep in dem woods a couple hours and then dey turn'em loose. When the boys came back tuh the house untouched, we fell on our knees wit thanks tuh the Lord dat dey didn't do nothin' to'em. In the end, dat Sheriff know *Blood Is Thicker Than Color,"* Baby Girl ended with a release of breath and burden.

Jack filled the air with his regret, "I's didn't mean tuh brang no harm tuh my fam'ly; Everythang just happened so fast."

Baby Girl attempted to soothe his worry. "Well, Papa was relieved tuh hear dat you made it tuh Uncle Lonnie's. We all wuz."

"Yep, I made it tuh Uncle Lonnie's. I had tuh get outta Mississippi. You know dat Sheriff can't stand none'a us, 'specially me. After the shootout, I crept back tuh the house where I found Norman. He took me to Greenwood and I hopped on the freight train."

"Yeah, Norman told us what happened. We's glad everythang's keen.

Bessie added, "Church ain't been the same, since dat day. It hurts my heart that Alma Lark got caught in the crossfire. Her husband stop comin' tuh the church, but the Reverend pray for her and her fam'ly every Sunday. We all prayin' for her and the fam'ly." Ella began to understand more and more why her mother and father did not want her to go South.

Everyone took time to ease back into the atmosphere, comfort and appreciation of home and family. Jack and his family had moved to the other side of the room. Baby Girl, Jake, Mary and Ella were still conversing at the table. At this time, Baby Girl expressed her desire to live in Chicago to Mary and Jake. Taking a deep breath, "You know, Mary and Jake, I been thanking I could live in a big city like dis, at least wit my family close by. Would it be okay tuh live here a little while wit yo fam'ly, until I can move out on my own? Ella smiled taking kindly to this idea and viewing Baby Girl as her own big sister.

Mary, with some concern, asked Baby Girl, "You thank Papa gonna be okay wit dis, wit him needing yo help and all?"

"Papa be fine. He got enough sharecroppers tuh help him. He really don't need me tuh work the farm."

Taking a few minutes alone to consider Baby Girl's request, Jake and Mary came to a final agreement and readily welcomed her into their family home. Baby Girl, with a smile thanked them both and moved toward Bessie and Jack to tell them of her new living arrangements. Jake excused himself so he could focus on the holiday pig that he was roasting.

Mary brought up the subject of employment for Baby Girl. "Baby Girl can get work in one of the houses, cleaning and taking care'a young'uns."

Baby Girl thought this was a good Idea, but she really had her mind set on the Cabaret. She was moving to big city and planning to shoot for the stars. "I ain't plan tuh be watch'n no mo' young'uns. I wanna sang and jig in the Cabaret, till I can get on the big scrang."

A sudden change of mood came into the room and turned all their faces into quiet, solemn expressions. Jack's face went pale; he wasn't too keen about this idea. Everybody seem to take a unified deep breath. Neither keeping house nor babysitting was on Baby Girl's agenda. She knew that she had the gift of a wonderful voice and boy could she dance a jig. She was every bit of a woman with a mind of her own. "Y'all know how much I love tuh sang and I'd make a great hoofer."

Afraid that his baby sister could end up as a Flapper working for the mafia, Jack replied, "Yep, dat melody coming from yo chops was sent from the heavens and yo feet do glide across the floor. Ain't no doubt 'bout that so I'll take you out jigging anytime you's wanna go."

Baby Girl looked disapprovingly at the group, but she could tell by the tone in Jack's voice that he was seriously, concerned, as her older brother about her welfare, so she agreed with some reluctance to ease their apprehensions.

Attempting to lighten the mood, Baby Girl asked, “Mary, let’s put on some music. I feel like cuttin’ a rug.” Mary laughingly agreed and found some dancing music to put on the phonograph. When the music started, Baby Girl grabbed Jack by the hand and commenced to jigging.

Chapter 11

The next day was Labor Day and the entire Brewer clan met at Mary's place. Jake's roasted pig had been sliced up and placed in the center of the table; everything looked and smelled fantastic. Mary and Baby Girl were a little weary from all the food preparations of smothered potatoes, macaroni and cheese, turnip greens, fried chicken, Jake's roasted pig, corn on the cob, waldorf salad and apple pie. They sat together at Jake's exquisitely crafted table and bowed their heads to pray and give thanks for their good fortune. Plates were filled and talk turned into moans and compliments on the magnificent meal as the family enjoyed the food.

After eating, they moved about the apartment laughing, talking and listening to the radio, all but Paul, who continued to sit at the table. He lit up a cigarette and took a puff; then he pulled his harmonica from a tiny velvet sack and started to blow a few bars.

Talking to Jack and Bessie, across the room Mary asked, "Where y'all stay last night?"

"We got a room between here and the boarding house, over on Michigan," Jack replied. I needed to get some fresh clothen from the boarding house dis morning, so I got up and went by the place. I got clanged up while I was dhere. I's wanted to get in and out, befo' Mrs. Smith -- dat's the woman dat run the establishment -- got up. I didn't wanna run into her asking me questions about where I been and where I'm going. Den I went back tuh the hotel and got Bessie and Earl."

Bessie commented, "Chicago a mighty fine city. Dey got a lot'a dem big boilers. What y'all call'um? Streetcars?"

Mary responded proudly like a person born and raised in the city. "Chicago got streetcars, trolley cars and motor buses. You can really get around up here although you know we not allowed tuh go all over the city. Our folks stay mainly right here in dis part of town. Dey got dividing lines and you might get killed, if you cross one. Dhere's an amusement park not too far from here called White City."

Jack asked in disbelief, "For crying out loud, you mean it's just for the White folks?"

"Yep, it's for the White folks. The place got all white buildings and the train take you right tuh it. I hear dem White folks spatting bout it at work. It's up there on 63rd Street, what dey call the Greater Grand Crossing area."

"Well, I'm going over dhere." Jack often forgot that he was a Negro man, pretending to be a white man, living in a segregated world.

“Jack, man, don't go gettin' in tuh no trouble now”, Paul barked. “You's already on the lam. We's don't need no trouble in Chicago.”

Baby Girl, sensing the tension about to rise changed the conversation, “I heard dis city be mighty fine at Christmas time. I’mo see for myself. I plans tuh move and be settled in Chicago way befo' Christmas.” Hearing that made Ella smile. She was looking forward to spending that time with her new “big sister.”

Mary voiced her approval. “I thank it’s gonna be just fine having Baby Girl here. Bessie, you's sho’ you gonna be able tuh manage wit out'a?”

I's get by, cuz dhere’s plenty folks back home tuh help wit the twins and Earl, but I'm gonna miss Baby Girl. The twins gonna mis'a too,” Bessie replied.

Mary then turned to look at her husband Jake, who had fallen asleep in the rocking chair. “Jake tired, he been working hard. Dey doing a lot building over on Indiana Street,” she added.

Meanwhile, Ella and Baby Girl played a game of dice. Ella was winning big, so big that Baby Girl had to comment, “I thank you double-cross me Ella. Where you learn tuh throw dose dice like dat?”

Papa show me how tuh throw these dice. He said he use to be the best dice thrower on his Beat. Now, I'm the best dice thrower,” she said with her gorgeous smile and stammering giggles. Ella didn't have much of a southern tongue. What she did have came from her southern parents.

Jack sat on the couch with his arm around Bessie who cradled Earl in her arms. Taking it all in Jack felt a deep comfort being in Chicago with his family, a feeling he had not experienced for some time. He savored the moment with his wife and baby. He felt carefree like he was on floating clouds in the sky. Jack did have remorse over what had happened to Alma Lark, the woman who was killed in the crossfire in the shootout between him and the Sheriff, but he was relieved that he had survived to be here to enjoy this time with his family.

Jake woke from his nap, stretched his arms and legs as he rose from the chair. “How about some manly refreshments?’ he said walking toward the wood cabinet that matched the beautifully carved table and chairs. He opened the doors to the top shelves, broke out the hooch and set glasses on the table. Jack checked with Bessie, who nodded her approval, before he left her and Earl to join Jake and his brother Paul at the table. Paul continued to blow his harmonica along with the phonograph music, and Baby Girl and Ella, who was almost as good a hoofer as her aunt, danced a jig together.

Before the night was over, Jack promised to take Bessie, Baby Girl and Ella to the picture palace. Ella did remind her Uncle Jack about the importance of school, which was at the top of list -- for now.

Chapter 12

Jack and Bessie met Baby Girl at the picture palace on 47th near South Parkway Boulevard around two o'clock. Baby Girl asked, "Dey don't show nothin' but films in dis here establishment?"

"Nope, nothin' but films", Jack responded. Dey got lot's establishments like dis in Chicago and dis one belong tuh us. Ain't no Peckerwoods up in here."

Jack bought three tickets to the palace. They entered and he politely proceeded to the john. Baby Girl and Bessie stood there taking notice of the small concession stand, located about thirty feet away. Neither of them had an interest in the partaking of snacks.

Jack came out the john, strutting in his zoot suit that he had purchased off Maxwell Street. He looked rather nifty in his new suit. It was a dark brown two piece suit. The jacket had large lapels with three large black buttons down the middle. He wore it with a white shirt and brown suspenders. Jack always wore suspenders with his trousers. He also wore a brown fedora with a wide brown ribbon that outlined the dome on his hat. Jack always wore a hat, just like his Uncle Lonnie told him to.

The suit was rather plain for a zoot suit, nothing resembling a gangster. Jack didn't want to be too flashy, but his fedora was Al Capone cold. Jack figured he'd get a lot of wear out of this fedora. Plus, he wanted to look good for the ladies, so he had concluded that it was worth spending some extra dough.

Bessie and Baby Girl were all dolled up for their day in the big city. Bessie had on a black cloche hat, empire-line style black dress which ended mid-legs. She had a protruding belly leftover from the young'uns. This style of dress really flattered her and since Bessie possessed such a large bosom, men didn't pay much attention to the rest of her body. Her hair was short and coarse, but you didn't see much of it underneath her stylish cloche. Bessie was out to enjoy herself. She hadn't been in Jack's company for many months and she didn't have to deal with the kids. Bessie was ready to be in the company of some live wires.

Baby Girl had on a red sheath style long sleeved dress that accented her curvy body. It had black trim around its round neck and waist. It was a bit shorter than Bessie's dress and she had the legs to go with it. She also had on a red loosely knitted headband, which looked stunting with her wave hairdo. They were some spiffy looking folks.

The Southside of Chicago is where the Negroes lived. Jack and Baby Girl could pass for white, but Bessie couldn't. It was hard to enjoy yourself as a Negro, outside of the neighborhood. Negroes couldn't even try on clothing in downtown Chicago. Clothing for Negroes was best explored on the Southside.

The picture room at the palace was large and held about five hundred folks. It contained an enormous breathtaking screen. There weren't many folks in the palace_ about eighty_ and Jack was joyful about this. It was Tuesday afternoon and the picture palace was quiet. Jack was content with this. He figured the fewer people, the better. This is why he had chosen to see the film during the daylight hours and early week. His desire was to take Bessie and Baby Girl out on the town and not be looking over his shoulder all the time. Bessie looked up at the walloping ceiling. The width, height and depth of the room gave it gigantic power. She thought it might take ten people or more standing on top of each other to touch the ceiling. They were standing in the old Apollo Theater. The name had been changed to Earl Theater in 1920.

The picture palace featured a film written, produced and directed by Oscar Micheaux. He was a well known Negro filmmaker, producer and director. He produced over forty films. Oscar Micheaux was born in Metropolis, Illinois in 1884. He moved to Chicago around 1901 and worked as a Pullman Porter. This is where he gained his worldly knowledge and a better understanding of business. Oscar Micheaux bought land in South Dakota in 1905. This is where he gained his inspiration for his first book, "The Conquest: The Story of a Negro Pioneer". He wrote and published it anonymously in 1913. Micheaux rewrote this book and self-published it as "The Homesteader" in 1917. It was basically an autobiography. The protagonist in the story was named Oscar Devereaux. Devereaux possessed a similar spelling to Micheaux. Oscar Micheaux wrote seven novels. "The Homesteader" was made into a film in 1919.

Jack, Baby Girl and Bessie were about to embark upon Oscar Micheaux's film titled "Body and Soul". It was a black and white silent film with script. This film was actually a little like Jack's life. The storyline was about an escaped prisoner seeking refuge in a primarily Negro town in Georgia and passing himself off as a Reverend.

Films produced by Negroes didn't play in the White folks' picture palaces and of course the White folks' films didn't play in the Negroes' picture palaces.

Jack had taken in several movies since he moved to Chicago; all of them were viewed at the white folks' picture palaces. He didn't have much to do during the week at the boarding house and films helped him pass the time. There was no need to come all the way south, since he was passing for white. He just went to the white folks' picture place. He was also a ladies' man, not much for being in a monogamous relationship. Jack loved Bessie and their children dearly, but he also loved the company of a broad. Jack didn't know what it meant to be loyal to one woman. This just wasn't in his blood. Jack was probably more like his Papa John Brewer than any of his brothers.

Papa John Brewer was always chasing the women. Jack had a good idea where his Papa was the night the Sheriff came to the house and dragged his brothers James and Norman out into the woods. He knew his papa was probably somewhere with a broad.

For a brief moment, Jack thought about Jennie back in Mississippi and their wild night of passionate nookie. His encounter with Jennie happened eight hours after his life ominous moment with the Sheriff. There he was eight hours later making whoopee with a woman other than Bessie.

Jack would enjoy Bessie while she was in town, but he would enjoy some other women while she wasn't in town. He figured what Bessie didn't know wouldn't hurt her. He figured his sisters already knew about his excursions; they knew their brothers. Jack was no exception. He would definitely have some squeeze.

Chapter 13

Upon leaving the picture palace, there were bright lights at a distance. As they strolled toward the lights, they noticed folks making their way in that direction. When they got closer to the reflecting lights, there was a carnival farther down on 47th Street.

Jack spoke, “What y'all wanna do now? We in our neighborhood. Fifty-fifth to Thirty-fifth Street, State Street to Cottage Grove, nothin' but Colored folks. We on 47th Street. We can do whatever we want. Dhere's all kind'a places round here.

“I's kind'a hungry and could use some viddles”, Bessie responded.

Baby Girl commented, “I'm hungry too.”

“I know where we can get some good viddles, listen tuh music and get a little hooch. We need tuh hop the streetcar. Dhere's a place over here on 35th and State Street called the Dreamland Cafe. I's read bout duh place in the Chicago Defender. I thank you's can get the Chicago Defender in Jackson. Dis the Colored newspaper. We's gonna have a good time.”

Baby Girl replied, "Let's get a wiggle on."

They patiently waited for the motor bus. After about ten minutes, the double-decker bus arrived. Thank goodness there was room on the top deck. There were two white folks standing at the stop with them. This was a new experience for Jack. He hadn't been forced to ride on the top of the bus or be faced with not being able to ride the bus, since he became Wade Johnson, the white man from Georgia.

At this moment, Jack felt like he was back in the South. He became overwhelmed with emotion, as he went deeper into his thought process. As his thoughts deepened about racism, he got angry. Bessie interrupted his anger. She whispered at Jack, "Ain't many of us on dis bus."

Jack responded, "Dhere's some buses dats just for us and most folks prefer tuh ride dem."

***

The Dreamland Cafe had a twenty-five cents cover-charge. Jack paid the seventy-five cents and they entered the club. It was nothing like the shine boxes back home in BlackHawk, Mississippi. It was spacious and elegant, possessing elongated tables with seating for ten. The room held about thirty of these tables. In the front of the room, there was a large elevated platform. You could see all the musicians and performers from anywhere on the ground level and white tablecloths dressed every table. The waiters dressed in formal attire, which consisted of short white suit jackets, white shirts and black slacks and black bow-ties.

It was about six-thirty and there was chatter that Alberta Hunter would be performing at seven. Jack had read about Alberta Hunter in the Chicago Defender. Jack did a lot of reading in his spare time. He became excited about possibly hearing her perform.

"You mean Alberta Hunter gonna be here. I's read about her in the newspaper. Dey say she can sang some jazz and blues. She used to perform at dis Dreamland Cafe all the time in the early twenties. We's should see bout some viddles. I seen some folks eating fried chicken and potatoes. We can get some chicken and potatoes."

Bessie commented, "I's want somethin' tuh drank. I's want some noodle juice."

Baby Girl chimed in, “I's don't want no noodle juice. Thank I'm gonna have a little giggle water. I knows dey got some. I got some dough, if you don't have enough Jack. Dis place is ritzy.”

There was plenty of giggle water to go around. Prohibition had driven down the price of booze.

Jack replied, “Dis keen, you got some scratch?”

“Papa gave me some dough. He wanted tuh make sure we had a good time.”

Jack responded, “So you could'a paid for us tuh get in? How much Papa give you?”

“Mind yo potatoes.”

A waiter came to the table and took their order for vittles and drinks. An announcement was made that Alberta Hunter would be performing around seven-thirty. Ms. Hunter had already traveled the world, performing in New York, Paris and London. This would be a treat seeing a performer of her stature.

Alberta Hunter was twelve years old when she left Memphis headed for Chicago. Her professional career started in Chicago at Dago Frank's, on the Southside in 1911. It was a rather rough establishment frequented by criminals and pimps, which closed down after a murder took place, two years later.

Folks were on the dance floor jigging, as they awaited Alberta Hunter's performance. This was Baby Girl's world. This was the world that she wanted to live in___singing and jigging in Chicago. This was her kind of city.

Chapter 14

Bessie, Earl and Baby Girl departed for Mississippi Wednesday around eleven in the morning. Jack thought that it would be nice, if they partook in a meal before they reached Union Station. There was a modish diner close to the station; so they hopped the trolley. This placed them a few blocks from Union Station and across the street from the diner. Jack had gone past Larry's Home Cooking Diner on several occasions. The restaurant stayed busy, so he figured the food must be tasty. It would be numerous hours before the ladies made it back home to BlackHawk. Mary had fried chicken for their trip and it was neatly packed in their luggage. Jack thought it might be better, if they ate something now.

Entering the chatter of the crowded diner, you could hear the clanging of the eating utensils against the platters and bowls. The laughter, giggles and the aroma of fine cuisine filled the air in the diner.

There was one section against the back wall that had been designated for Negroes. The four of them found a booth in the segregated section. They made themselves comfortable as they waited for the waitress to come. The diner didn't have your typical four legged tables. Larry's had wooden top tables, covered with white and silver vinyl, trimmed in a silver metallic with pole centers, which sat upon a plated metal bottom that formed an X. There were wooden booths and tables lining the outer walls, which is the section they were seated in. There was also a soda-fountain counter. The establishment had been wallpapered in a floral print.

Jack started the conversation. “It was mighty fine seeing y'all. I'm glad everythang worked out. Please thank Papa for helping wit the trip. Bessie, you know I's gonna make thangs right. I just need a little mo time. Give the twins a hug and kiss for me.”

Bessie commented, “It's just hard right now. I's know thangs gonna work out; dey always do.”

Baby Girl chimed in, “Jack, I'm gon'na see you soon. I's moving tuh Chicago. I'll be here befo' Christmas. I's wanna help Papa and Bessie get some thangs setdled back home and den I's coming.”

The waitress came to their table and quietly took orders. They all ordered sandwiches with a pop. Baby Girl and Bessie didn't want to eat a big meal. Mary had fried chicken so they would have something to eat. It wouldn't spoil during their long ride home.

Jack sat at the table cradling Earl, trying to discover some resemblance of himself. He fiddled with Earl's fingers and brushed his cheeks with the back of his hand. Earl stared up at Jack with his little brown eyes, grinning like he possibility knew who Jack was.

Some Colored folks came and sat down close by. They mentioned the city of LeFlore. He immediately thought LeFlore, Mississippi, which wasn't far from BlackHawk. The couple gave Jack a second glance, as though he looked familiar. He quickly turned his face towards the wall and cocked his hat down on one side.

Now Jack was paranoid. He pushed Bessie and Baby Girl to quickly finish their meals, so they could head for the train station.

***

Upon entering the train station, there was a feeling of solitude. It appeared as though the correct time had been chosen for departure and this warmed Jack's bones. They quickly found a bench to park their carcasses. A newspaper laid on the bench, which Jack quickly picked up and commenced to scrutinizing it.

He obtained great joy from the comic section of the paper.

Baby Girl said, “I'll send you a telegram, so you's can meet me here at the station.”

Jack replied, “Bessie, I wish you and the twins could come too, but we need a place tuh stay. Like I said befo', I need a little mo time.”

“Jack you just take care'a thangs here. I's can handle thangs back home”, Bessie replied. “We miss you, but we'll manage. I'm thanking bout finding a new church for the New Year. I's just can't take how folks look at us during service.”

“I's know its hard right now, but it's gonna get better. You got my word.”

There was an announcement that their train was boarding. Jack gave the two of them colossal hugs. Bessie also got a gigantic kiss in the kisser. Jack told her that he loved her and that he sent his love to the family.

They boarded the train and Jack stood by until the train departed. He made his way back to the boarding house. Jack needed to give Mrs. Smith some dough. He had spent a lot of scratch during their visit. He had also given Mary some money to help with the holiday feast. This meant Jack would need to put in overtime at the mill, so he could replenish his dough.

He laid in bed pondering over how to be with his family. The twins were growing-up fast and this sadden him. He truly wanted to be with his boys. Jack mulled on his situation for a while. There had to be a better solution. This wasn't the type of papa that he had envisioned himself to be. He decided that if he worked hard at correcting the problem that he might be able to get Bessie and the twins in Chicago by the spring.

Chapter 15

Winter was coming in full-force and it was reflected through the leaves now covering the ground. Jack had received one letter from Bessie in recent days. Thanksgiving was a couple of days away and he would be going over to Mary's. Baby Girl would be there to join in the celebration. Jack was anticipating the Thanksgiving Day Supper.

The following day, Jack met Baby Girl at the train station. He reminded Baby Girl that he was going by the name Wade Johnson and it would be greatly appreciated, if she referred to him by this name in public. She agreed to call him Wade when they were in the company of others.

Baby Girl let Jack know that it would be a long time before he could come back to Mississippi. "Dat Sheriff Rodgers is just like a hound dog. He ain't lost his scent for you. He come by the house all times a day, hunting for clues. Dat Sheriff giving everybody a hard time, but we's glad you got away."

Jack knew Mary had worked earlier and didn't want to impose on her, by bringing Baby Girl to the house hungry. They stopped off at Larry's Home Cooking Diner once again. This was the same diner that they had eaten at during Baby Girl's and Bessie's departure Labor Day. They entered Larry's and placed Baby Girl's luggage in the designated luggage area, which was for whites only. The restaurant being in close proximity to the train station created patrons with much luggage. This time they didn't sit in the Negro section of the diner. Both of them could pass for white. They sat down at the soda-fountain counter and ordered something to drink. You could also eat at the counter, as long as you ordered an ice cream of some sort.

Jack had his hat on as usual. He had accumulated several hats, since coming to Chicago. He was sporting the fedora that he had purchased on Maxwell St. Jack was trying to keep his head down and his face hidden. He had noticed that the diner was a hot-spot for the railroad workers. They had great food and the news of good food traveled far. People seem to be coming from all over the place to eat at this diner. Jack prayed that no one recognized him.

He noticed that there was a "Help Wanted" sign in the window. He suggested that Baby Girl inquire about this work.

Baby Girl asked the waitress, "The sign in the window say y'all looking for help? Who can I speak wit bout dis?"

“You'd need to speak with Mr. Calhoun. He is the man over there with the plaid shirt. He is speaking to the woman with the flowered hat.”

“Thank you.”

They ordered some food and waited for Mr. Calhoun to finish speaking with the lady. Baby Girl waved her arm at Mr. Calhoun, making eye to eye contact with him and gesturing that she needed his attention. Jack decided that this would be a good time to take a leak. He removed himself from the counter and found the white only john. Mr. Calhoun came swaggering over to the counter.

“Hello Ma'am. I'm Mr. Calhoun and this is my fine establishment. What can I do for you?

Baby Girl looked into this short bald man's beady eyes. “Mr. Calhoun. You seem to be looking for help. I's new in town and looking for work. I's can start right after the holiday.”

“Well now. Where you here from?”

“I's from Georgia and been traveling for two days now. I's mighty tired." Baby Girl announced as she batted her eyes at Mr. Calhoun.

Baby Girl was a gorgeous breathtaking woman. Mr. Calhoun was a little smitten with Baby Girl. He didn't have a clue that she was a Colored. He had Negroes working in his establishment. They worked mostly in the kitchen, with the exception of a few Negro waitresses working the Colored tables. Baby Girl knew that Mr. Calhoun thought she was a white woman. She decided to let him keep thinking this.

Mr. Calhoun commented, "Ah, Georgia, a mighty fine state and you are a lovely Georgian. Madam, as you can see, we are quite busy. I am in need of a few more ladies to work the tables. Most of your wages will be made off the tables, but as you can see, we keep a full house. This establishment will be closed for Thanksgiving. You may start the following Saturday and work all weekend. Be here Saturday morning around seven."

"Well, Mr. Calhoun, I's thank you. I'll be here", Baby Girl responded with her sexy smile.

After Mr. Calhoun finished speaking with Baby Girl, Jack returned to the counter. The waitress had delivered their turkey sandwiches. They both took heaping bites. “So what he say?”

“He said dat I's could start Saturday after the holiday. I'll be working all weekend.”

“Dis keen. You'll be making nifty dough in dis place. Look at all dees folks. Dis place like dis all the time.”

They finished their food, grabbed the luggage and headed for Mary's place. Arriving an hour later, Paul answered the door. He gave Baby Girl a sizable hug and they plunked her luggage over by the window in the front room.

Paul barked, “How was the trip? How's thangs back home? Papa holding up okay?”

“The trip was fine. I'm a little tired wit packing and all. Papa doing swell. He talking bout getting rid of some acres, but I thank he full'a baloney.”

Jack chimed in, “Where's everybody? Dey in the back?”

"Yep. Dey back dhere. Mary just got home from work, not too long ago. I thank Jake taking a nap. Ella went over tuh the market. Sit down and rest yourself. I thank Mary wanna cook some catfish."

Mary entered from the back room. She gave Baby Girl and Jack a kiss on the cheek. Jack and Baby Girl were seated on the couch. Paul was daydreaming out the window. Mary plopped herself in the rocking chair. "Oh-hhh...... I'm tired. Dey been working me hard. I had tuh start branging work home. I need tuh finish dees orders befo' Christmas. It be here befo' we's know it. White folks always want new dresses for Christmas and New Year's. I's really busy at work dis time'a year. I's been working for Mis'ez Wilson roundabout seven years now, so she let me brang thangs home during the holiday season."

Paul broke out of his daydreaming. "Mis'ez Wilson done built herself a fine establishment, since Mary been sewing fo'a."

"Just a little somethin' Mama taught me. It help keep food on the table."

Ella enters with the catfish from the market. She had a big smile on her face upon seeing Baby Girl had returned from Mississippi with substantial baggage. Baby Girl winked at Ella. She began to giggle.

Jack said, “Baby Girl picked up some work on duh way in. Dey need help over at the diner by the train depot. We's stopped in dhere on the way over here and grabbed some viddles. She gonna be waiting tables. I figured Mary be tired and Baby Girl be empty-bellied.”

“I'm tired, but I's still gotta fix some viddles for Ella and Jake. Ella can help me. Dis why I's sent huh tuh the market. Fish don't take no time tuh cook.”

Baby Girl was falling asleep on the couch, so Mary lightly placed a blanket over her. Paul and Jack decided to move into the kitchen, so they wouldn't disturb Baby Girl. They also wanted to drink hooch, while Mary fried the fish up. Ella decided to relax in the rocking chair, which was positioned close to Baby Girl in the front room. She read her book quietly, as she kept an eye on her aunt, with the fireplace burning softly.

Chapter 16

Mary and Baby Girl prepared a feast for Thanksgiving. They both enjoyed cooking and were happy to cook for such a special occasion. Their preparations consisted of smothered chicken, dressing, candied sweet potatoes, macaroni and cheese, collard greens, fried corn, blackeyed peas, peach cobbler, bread pudding and sweet potato pie.

When Jack arrived for his Thanksgiving feast, Paul and Jake were in the corner of the front room shooting craps by the window. Jake appeared to be winning. Ella was sitting in Jake's rocking chair, which had been moved close to the crap game. Ella thought the crap game between her Uncle Paul and her Papa was funny. She knew her Papa had been the best dice thrower on his Beat back home. Mary and Baby Girl were getting the vittles on the table. It appeared as though Jack was right on time to eat and he was starving. He hadn't eaten since yesterday afternoon. He had saved his appetite. Mary called everyone to the table.

“Y'all come get dees viddles, while dey hot. Let’s say a prayer first.”

They stood around the table holding hands, as they all spoke in unison, “God is great, God is good, Let us thank him fo' dis food. Ah'man.”

They all grabbed a chair around the table for eight and started piling food onto their dishes. Everything tasted so good. There wasn't much talking during supper. Jack really appreciated the bread pudding. It was made just the way his mama use to make it, with cinnamon and lots of raisins. “Dis bread pudding sho is good. It taste just duh way mama use tuh make it. It's been a long time since I had bread pudding like dis.”

Mary responded, “I showed Baby Girl how tuh make it. Now she know how mama use tuh make it. Ella know too.

Paul commented, “Dis peach cobbler is keen. I's had a taste for cobbler.”

Baby Girl spoke while winking at Ella. “Glad y'all like the viddles. Ella helped wit the viddles too.”

Ella just giggled. She hadn't actually cooked any of the vittles. She had cut up potatoes and picked and cleaned greens. After dinner they sat around talking and listening to the radio.

***

Meanwhile, back in Mississippi, Jennie was about to have Jack's baby. Jack didn't try to contact Jennie anymore after he left the South. He figured her husband had to be off the chain-gang. They were both married and that night should have never happened.

Jennie had the baby about five days after Thanksgiving. Her husband took one look at the baby and he knew that it couldn't possibly be his child.

"Whose damn baby is dis?"

The baby was very light skinned. Wilbert had brown chocolate skin. He was thin and somewhat tall. Jennie was also brown skinned. She was a shorter woman with medium coarse hair. The baby's complexion was far lighter than either of theirs. None of their children were anywhere near this fair skinned. The baby also had light brown eyes.

Jennie told Wilbert, “It’s yo baby Wilbert.”

Wilbert wasn’t stupid. He knew this baby couldn’t possibly be his child. He knew that Jennie must have taken up relations with some other man. He was angry and this caused him to become physically and verbally abusive. He struck Jennie across her face.

The baby was named John, better known as Johnny. Johnny was given the family’s surname, so he was Johnny Johnson.

Jennie's life was even harder after little Johnny was born. Wilbert was already an angry and evil man. He became angrier and more violent. He didn’t have any choice, when it came to taking care of baby Johnny. Jennie dealt with his evil mood and protected her Johnny. She didn’t care who the baby’s papa was. This was her child. She loved him just like she loved the rest of her children. She didn’t care what Wilbert thought. Johnny was his child now. This was her story and she was sticking to it.

Chapter 17

Jack received a letter from Bessie around the first of December. She expressed that she would like to spend New Year's with him in Chicago and that she would be arriving a few days prior. She would provide him with additional information.

Jack was glad that Baby Girl had moved to Chicago, but he hadn't spent much time with her since her arrival. He had been putting in overtime at the steel mill and she worked fluctuating hours at the diner.

Jack and Baby Girl were about to experience their first Chicago Christmas. Jack was getting into the holiday spirit, by humming Christmas lullabies, but on Christmas Day there was ten inches of snow on the ground. It was a real Chicago winter.

Jack stayed at the boarding house Christmas Day. He didn't even try to go see his siblings. This was his first Christmas without his family. Mrs. Smith had the dining room decorated beautifully. She was very handy with her hands and loved to bake.

Mrs. Smith had made Christmas ornaments for the tree. She had also prepared a small Christmas dinner for the tenants, nothing fancy, just some breaded chicken, a small ham, mash potatoes and asparagus. Mrs Smith had anticipated a snowstorm based on her years of living in Chicago. She had also baked cookies. It actually turned out to be a wonderful Christmas.

Jack sat around the house with Mrs. Smith and a couple of the other Boarders. They drank spiked hot cider, as they listened to the radio and talked. Jack told lots of lies about growing up in Georgia. He was starting to grow into this Wade character.

Jack told a story about him and his Papa down by the river back home.... "See my Papa own a small fishing boat. One day we had the boat down out in the river. We's trying tuh do a little fishing, when I's spotted somethin' in the water. I's knew it was a gator by way the water was moving, so I's told my Papa tuh hand me the big net dat was behind him.." Jack told many lies this day. He was starting too really like being *Wade*. Wade could be whatever and whomever he wanted Wade to be.

Chapter 18

1927 wasn't just bringing in a New Year. It was bringing Bessie to Chicago. Jack was extremely excited about being in Chicago with Bessie and Baby Girl for the New Year. He decided that they would venture Downtown. Jack planned to sport the zoot suit that he purchased off Maxwell Street. Bessie was arriving today, Thursday and New Year's Eve would be on Saturday.

Jack met Bessie at Union Station. They took the streetcar to a hotel. Bessie had left the young'uns in Mississippi. Neither one of them could wait to get the other one alone. The hotel had five floors and their room was located on the third. When they entered the quaint looking hotel, they walked straight on to the elevator. The elevator operator was a young Colored fellow dressed in black slacks, red vest and white shirt. He wasn't very neighborly and this was just fine with Bessie and Jack. The operator closed the metal gate style door and cranked the handle located on the wall of the elevator which took Jack and Bessie to their floor.

As they entered the drab but clean hotel room, Jack started to dismantle his clothing. He threw his fedora in the chair that was seated by the window. Then he pulled Bessie close to him and started to help her out of her clothing, while nibbling on her ear.

She started running her fingers through Jack's hair. Bessie had a corset on, which slowed them down just briefly. Jack helped her get out of it quickly, as he kissed, licked and sucked all over her body. It was passionate uproarious merrymaking on and off, for the next twenty-four hours.

***

Jack and Bessie headed out on the town New Year's Eve around seven o'clock. Jack had heard about the wonderful lights and window displays in downtown Chicago. He envisioned walking the streets in downtown Chicago with Bessie's arm wrapped around his. Jack had heard how wonderful Chicago was this time of year and wanted to see the department store windows on State Street. They hopped the motor bus heading downtown with the anticipation of experiencing the *Big City.*

Once they arrived downtown, the streets were congested with boilers, motor buses, streetcars and all the people. They got off the streetcar in front of Marshall Field's & Co. There were street vendors selling hot cider and coffee in various locations along State Street. They purchased something to drink, while they waited for Baby Girl to arrive.

“Look at all the lights”, Bessie squawked. “Folks all dolled-up and dees establishments mighty swanky.”

After about twenty minutes Baby Girl was standing in front of Marshall Field's. Bessie and Jack connected with her and Baby Girl spatted "Dees some ritzy looking folks down here, look at all the lights. What y'all wanna do? How I look? I might meet my husband..."

Bessie started laughing and responded, "You's just might, but dhere's a lot folks out here. Dis might not be the bess place tuh meet no gentleman caller".

Jack spatted, "You's just gonna be an old spinster".

Baby Girl didn't take to Jack's words too kindly. She gave him a scowling look, but decided that he wasn't going to ruin her New Year. Baby Girl was out to find her a husband in this New Year.

They stared into Marshall Field's exquisitely decorated window displays. One display was lit with colorful, white, yellow, red, green and blue lights. It displayed toy soldiers with riffles. There were toys and gifts underneath a finely decorated tree, along with Santa Claus. There were figurines of children demonstrating joyful faces. The images of the people had a realistic quality about them. You could tell that every piece had been handcrafted.

"Jack, dat soldier right dare look just like you", Baby Girl pronounced with a little giggle in her voice.

Jack whispered, "If he what'n white, he might just look like me."

Bessie chimed in, "Mis'ta Smith over on Beat 2 know how tuh make toys like dat. Let's get a wiggle on; it's nippy out here." It was actually a beautiful night, considering that they were in Chicago and it was thirty-eight degrees. Most of the snow that fell for Christmas had already melted. Jack replied, "Folks puttin' on duh Ritz."

They decided that since it was a New Year *and* Jack wasn't on the chain-gang or dead, fun was definitely on the menu. They wanted to live life to the fullest. Baby Girl and Jack had already lost their oldest sibling named Jerusha. She had been passing for white and dating a white man. Jerusha got knocked-up and the baby came out looking like the Negro she was. The white man killed her and left her body in the family yard. Jack and Baby Girl realized they could be dead at any moment, pretending to be White folks. They prayed not to run in to anybody they knew, especially since Bessie was with them. She couldn't pass for White. They would need to pretend that Bessie was a domestic servant out helping them for the holiday.

They looked at the people walking around enjoying themselves, as they awaited the New Year, while strolling down beautiful State Street. Baby Girl purchased herself a warm drink to help warm her bones.

Jack decided that since they were living dangerously, they should go to a speakeasy. A speakeasy for the Coloreds was called a *shine box*. A speakeasy served illegal alcohol and you could distinguish between the White and Colored clubs by the words *speakeasy* and *shine box*. *Shine box* deriving from Negroes being compared to *black shoe shine polish.*

All three of them were dressed elegantly, underneath their winter coats. Jack had bought Bessie a lovely long blue wool coat. This was her belated Christmas gift along with pointed-toed lace-up boots, which stopped midway her legs. Plus, Jack didn't want to waste a good shave and a fresh haircut.

The three of them had to leave downtown to get to a shine box. They just wanted to make it to a shine box before midnight. It was chilly standing at the stop waiting for the motor bus. Jack put his arms around Bessie to help keep her warm. There were several shine boxes on 35th Street. They would take the State Street bus straight down.

When they climbed into the motor bus, there were only two seats available. Baby Girl and Jack sat in those seats amongst the white folks. Bessie had to stand, because it wouldn't look right for Jack to stand, since Bessie was with them, with Jack looking white and all. They didn't want to take any chances, the night had gone well up to now. The bus ride was only twenty minutes.

Jack was taken-in upon entering the shine box. The Jazz was sounding great and folks were jiggling all over the place. The Club was lit-up with the New Year's spirit. There were snazzy little wooden tables with white and red feathered decorations sprouting from vases placed on each table. Strings of different colored beads of various sizes were also there. The beads had been provided for the ladies to wear around their necks, creating a feeling of festiveness. The women were all gorgeous and the gentlemen handsome. The place was filled with about two hundred people, swing dancing, tap dancing and just hoofing all over the club.

Jack could do the foxtrot a little bit, but there wasn't much fox-trotting going on at this joint. He wasn't very interested in jigging and didn't mind if Bessie did. She wasn't very interested in jigging either. Bessie just wanted to enjoy the music and have conversation with her husband. As usual, Jack wanted some hooch. He wanted to sit around and drink in his New Year, as he pretended to be hanging on to every word Bessie had to say.

There were several men checking Baby Girl out, as she sashayed across the floor to the john. She was the cat's meow in that dress Mary had made for her. The gentlemen in the club weren't the only ones checking out the merchandise. Baby Girl was doing some observing of her own.

She caught the eye of a good looking gentleman named Charles Watson. He was rather tall with golden brown skin and a deep dimple in his chin.

Baby Girl did look stunning in her red dress. It was a red silk flapper dress with beaded sequin around the bosom. The dress stopped mid-length down the legs, making her fabulous legs a real tease. She was a real dish that night. Baby Girl had even borrowed red shoes from Mary and placed a red rose in her hair.

Well, the clock struck midnight and the New Year came in. It was officially 1927. The hooping, hollering and kissing struck the entire joint. Jack grabbed Bessie and gave her a whopper of a kiss. Baby Girl was standing in the middle of the dance floor, when this man named Charles Watson stood in front of her. She thought, "It's a New Year and I's in Chicago. Dhere's a good looking hunk'a man standing in front'a me. Chicago is my kind'a city."

Charles spoke, “Happy New Year beautiful. Would you like tuh jig?”

Baby Girl's breath was taken away by this fine-looking gentleman. She couldn't say a word, as he grabbed her by the hand to jig. Baby Girl jigged with Charles several times, as they got to know each other in the New Year. They found themselves a table in the corner, alone, away from *Jack*. They kept their vision on each other, as they sipped on some giggle water.

Charles spoke, “So what you like tuh do Lucinda?”

“I love tuh jig. I wanna be a *hoofer* one day. I like dat picture palace too. You from Chicago? You don't sound like it. You's from the South. Where's bout?”

“I's from Butler County in Missouri. I's work over at duh Palm House.”

“Dat's a ritzy looking establishment. We just saw dat place downtown. I haven't been in Chicago long. You's didn't have tuh work tonight?”

“Nope, I's don't work for no white folks on New Year's Eve. I's work for dem all year long.”

"I's work over at Larry's Home Cooking Diner, by the train depot. I's come tuh Chicago right befo' Thanksgiving. I's got plenty kinfolk in Chicago. Lets jig some mo. You's a good hoofer."

Baby Girl and Charles danced a lot that night. The music slowed down, so Jack got Bessie to dance with him. He just wanted to get close to Charles and Baby Girl, while they were on the dance floor. Jack wanted to check Charles out. He thought Baby Girl might be getting a little smitten. Baby Girl introduced Charles to her brother *Wade* and her sister-in-law.

Jack spoke, "Nice tuh meet yuh. You from dees parts?" Jack didn't waste any time getting information out of Charles. He wanted as much information as he could get, as soon as he could get it. He wanted to make sure Charles wasn't mixed up with the Mob.

"My name Charles Watson. I's from Butler County in Missouri. Been here bout three years now."

Baby Girl stated with a stern voice, "Mind yo potatoes"

Bessie thought she'd help Jack out, "I'm thanking bout moving tuh Chicago. You's didn't have no problem finding work when you got here? What kind'a work you do?"

“I's work in duh kitchen over at duh Palm House. Deys got plenty of jobs in Chicago.”

Bessie responded, “Dat's one'a dos swanky hotels.”

Well by this time, they had jigged three tunes. This was enough jiggling for Jack. He had obtained enough information for now. He was satisfied with Charles credentials. They stayed at the shine box for several hours, departing around three o'clock.

***

Bessie left Chicago two days later, headed back to Mississippi. The weather in Chicago had taken a tremendous turn for the worst. She was glad to be returning south. This particular winter was nothing nice. Everyone had a hard time moving around the city. Jack only saw his siblings a couple times the rest of the winter. Baby Girl and Charles didn't seem to let the winter keep them apart. Charles was carrying a serious torch for Baby Girl.

Chapter 19

The worst of the Chicago Winter was over, leaving March with the presence of an early spring. Baby Girl was ready to connect with Jack, so she decided to stop by the boarding house. Mrs. Smith answered the door.

“Ma'am I's Lucinda Johnson. I's looking for my brother Wade Johnson.” Baby Girl decided to use the surname Johnson. She didn't want to arouse any suspicion in Mrs Smith.

“Well hello, come on in. I think Wade is here. His room is the third door on the left, down that hallway.”

“Thank you Ma'am.” Baby Girl knocked on Jack's door.

“What you doin' here? Is dhere a beef ?”

“No beef, I's wanted tuh see my brother. Been months, since I seen ya. Dat was a rough winter we's just had. Dis weather gonna take some gettin' use to.”

“How's the rest of the family? Everybody okay? ”

“Everybody keen. Let's go fo'a walk.”

This gave Jack and Baby Girl a chance to get caught up. Jack told Baby Girl all about the boarding house and the people that lived there. He told her about the Hobo's on the train and the advice that he had received from Uncle Lonnie. He talked about bringing Bessie and the kids to Chicago permanently, since he would never be able to return to Mississippi. Baby Girl wanted to know when he would send for them.

Jack stated, "I need tuh contact Papa. I could use his help. We'll need tuh find a place tuh stay. I'm gonna need tuh ponder on dis. I wonder what dat Sheriff Rodgers up to? I's don't need him tuh know dat Bessie and the kids leavin'. He probably figure dey knows where I am."

"You can't never speak on dis at work. Dey can't never meet Bessie. If dey do, deys gonna know you ain't one'a dem. Dey thank you sangle, just let'um keep thankin' it."

Jack and Baby Girl hopped the trolley over to Mary's on 39th in Michigan. After a half an hour on the trolley, they were at 35th in Michigan. They got off and walked the rest of the way. Jack hung out at Mary's place the rest of the day. He decided to spend the night. Jack, Baby Girl and Mary sat around talking all evening.

Baby Girl spoke, "I's wonder what James and Norman up to. Dey like tuh go fishing over in Coila.

Jack responded, “I's always like tuh go fishin' in Coila too. Dhere's a little river run not far from Rosebank Church. Dey got some nice fish.”

Mary chimed in, “I's don't miss nothin' in the South, but my family. Chicago is a keen city.”

***

Jack headed back to the boarding house the next morning, after stopping off for his lucky breakfast at Ethel's. It was Sunday afternoon and all was quiet at the boarding house. He went to his room and laid across the bed, wondering how it would be once Bessie and the young'uns came. Jack envisioned little feet running around and good smelling vittles coming from the stove. He pondered on how his young'uns wouldn't need to travel so far for their schooling. But he also thought about all the wonderful experiences that he had in the south growing up. Jack thought about his horse and how his papa would take him hunting in the woods. He also thought about the first time he roped, killed and roasted a pig.

Jack went to work the following day at the mill. He ate lunch with his co-worker at work as usual. He had the strongest desire to tell him about Bessie and the kids, but he knew that he couldn't. His co-worker was actually pretty cool for a peckerwood, but this was based on the fact that he thought Jack was peckerwood too. Jack wondered how his friend would treat him, if he had the knowledge that he was a Negro. Would he still want to be his friend? Would he turn him in for passing for white folk? Would he kill him? Jack wondered what the remainder of his life would be like as Wade Johnson.

The work week went by slowly. Jack had already decided to visit Paul and Mary on the weekend. He would visit Mary on Saturday and Paul on Sunday. He had to speak with them about bringing Bessie and the young'uns to Chicago.

***

In the meantime, back in Mississippi, Wilbert and Jennie were in the process of relocating. They had purchased forty acres of land in Missouri. Wilbert's heart was growing more evil every moment. Baby Johnny was a normal baby and getting bigger and bigger. Wilbert was still stewing over the fact that Johnny wasn't his young'un. "He ain't nun'a mine."

Sheriff Rodgers was a *one armed man* with a score to settle. He lived several miles away from the Brewer family home, but made it his duty to venture past the Brewer home, as often as possible.

The Sheriff was seeking any information that he could, regarding Jack's whereabouts.

Chapter 20

The following weekend, Jack went by to chat with Mary. When he arrived at the building unit, Mary was sweeping the stairs.

"What brang you round about dis way?"

"I's need tuh spill."

"I's reckin dat might be okay. Let's go inside. What's eatin' you'? Nobody here but me."

"No beef, everythang nifty. Baby Girl at work?"

"She wit Charles. I thank dey stuck together, but she really been helpin' out around here."

Jack responded, "Anybody heard from Papa? I's been thankin' bout brangin' Bessie and the young'uns here tuh live. I'm not so sure, dis a good idea?"

Mary commented, "I spoke wit Paul a coup'la days ago. He said dem wanted ads still round Mississippi and other parts. I don't thank its such a good idea tuh brang Bessie and the young'uns up dis way. You still a wanted man. Dis ain't no kind'a life for dem. You's passing for White and all..."

“I'm gonna go see Paul tomorrow and let him know my intentions.”

“You do dat! Talk tuh Paul bout it. Paul knows a guy, who can help y'all get a place tuh stay, if you insist on doin' dis. Nobody gonna wanna rent tuh y'all. You either gonna be passing or be what yuh are, Colored folk. Not gonna be easy findin' a place for y'all to live. Colored folks having a hard time findin' a place tuh stay.”

“I'll see Paul tomorrow. I'm goin' by after he come from church.”

"I's got some dough saved up, if you need some. Don't mention it tuh Jake. He don't know dat I got dis dough. Mama was always big on puttin' it away for a raining day.”

Jack smiled and gave Mary a kiss on the cheek as he departed. As Jack traveled back to the boarding house, he thought about Bessie, the twins and Baby Earl. He wanted to be with his family. He would never be able to return to the South.

Jack thought about the first time he formally met Bessie. They were at the farmers market. There she was dressed in an ocean blue colored dress, buying some strawberry preserves. He thought about when the twins were born and the twenty-two hours of intense labor that Bessie experienced. They had to call Sara May the midwife over. She had delivered Jack and all his siblings.

Jack felt saddened, as he reminisced about home. A tear dropped from his eyes. He had to rectify his problem. He couldn't spend the remainder of his life like this.

The following day Jack went to see Paul. When he arrived at Paul's place, he could hear the ball game on the radio. Jack knocked hard on the door.

"Jack, come on in. I's just got in from church, not too long ago. I'm trying tuh decide what tuh fix for supper. You stayin' for supper? You mo dan welcome. You spoke wit Mary lately?"

"I saw Mary yesterday. I stop by and we had a spill."

"You's gotta beef?"

"No beef, I wanna brang Bessie and the young'uns up here tuh live. I's been pondering whether dis a good idea. I really want dem here wit me, but its gonna be harder tuh hide. We's gonna need a place tuh stay. Mary mentioned dat you might be able tuh help us out. Mary don't thank its such a good idea, wit me bein' a wanted man and all."

"Mary told you right! I's know you love Bessie and the young'uns, but you not gonna get tuh be wit dem anytime soon. You still a wanted man. Its not fair tuh Bessie and the young'uns. You's looking over your shoulder all the time. Jack, you not gonna be able tuh go around wit dem, unless you gonna be *colored folk*. You's can't be tryin' tuh pass for white."

"Mary said you knew a man who might be able tuh help us out with a place tuh stay."

"I'll get in touch wit'um. When you plannin' do dis?"

"I need tuh talk wit Bessie first. She might not be up tuh travelin' right now, seeing she got the twins--- and Earl. Maybe Baby Girl can go tuh Mississippi and help dem move up here."

"You's not thankin' straight. Dhere's plenty folks back home tuh help Bessie. You know Papa will help, but you gonna have tuh talk tuh him yourself. You stayin' for supper?"

"Nope, I'm not stayin'. I wanna get back tuh the boardin' house. I'm little tired. I been puttin' in overtime and need tuh rest a spell. I need tuh ponder on dis some mo'."

“Alright, thanks fuh stoppin' by”.

Paul thought about Jack after he departed. He thought about all the stories that he had heard about Jack, when Jack was growing-up. Paul hadn't been around Jack much due to their age difference, but he had heard plenty of stories from back home. He thought about the time Jack let the neighbors' chickens out the coop and the honey he poured in Ray Jones rifle, because he threatened to kill the family’s hunting dog. Paul had himself a good laugh, as he thought about his baby brother Jack.

Chapter 21

It was mid-May and folks were squirming about in the city. The past winter made folks take advantage of the warm air that was starting to present itself, before the next winter settled in.

Jack resumed his normal routine of going back and forth between work and the boarding house. He was still eating his meals at Ethel's Place, as he waited for a response from a telegram that he sent Bessie. He continued his frequent visits to the picture palace. Jack had gotten lucky with the broads a couple of time at the picture palace and he didn't waste his time traveling to the Colored neighborhoods to go to a picture palace. Jack just went ahead and attended the White folks' picture palaces and sat in the white folks section. He figured what they didn't know wouldn't hurt them.

Around the beginning of June he got a letter from Bessie. She addressed her concerns over him passing for White. She let him know that she didn't want to come to Chicago to live at this time, but she would continue to visit. Bessie expressed that if they were going to be together, some changes would need to occur. She would let Jack know when she felt complacent about moving to Chicago.

Jack was sadden by Bessie's news that she didn't want to relocate north. This put him in the mood for hooch. He knew where a speakeasy was close to the boarding house. It was for peckerwoods only, but at this stage in his life, he figured it didn't matter who he drank with. He was passing for one of them anyway, so why not drink with them. He just wanted some hooch. Jack had loss his identity. He had loss his family. Jack had loss the state he grew-up in. He was starting to feel as though he had lost everything, even though he had survived the sheriff. Jack felt remorse over Alma Lark's death and hoped that the Lord would forgive him for being involved in this incident. He knew the Sheriff had loss his arm, but he felt that he had loss much more than that Sheriff. The Sheriff had another arm. He didn't have but one family. If Bessie didn't come back to Chicago with the young'uns, he might not ever see them again. He could never go south, never.

***

Jack went by Mary's place the following Sunday. He got together every third Sunday with his siblings for dinner. He wanted to let them know that he had heard from Bessie and that she did not wish to move at this time.

The entire Brewer clan was at Mary's, minus Charles for Sunday dinner. As they sat and ate around Jakes' table, Jack informed them of the response from his telegram to Bessie.

“I's heard back from Bessie, bout movin' tuh Chicago. She' don't wanna come right now. She'll just keep visit'n'.”

Baby Girl responded, “Jack give Bessie a little time. The twins still young and now she got Earl. Dats a lot'a folks tuh move and you leavin' so sudden and all.”

Jake chimed in, “It sho is ...It was hard when the three of us moved in dis here place. Ella was much younger at duh time.”

Jack and the family were able to speak freely about things, since Charles wasn't present. The family had never spoken about Jack's plight in front of Charles.

Chapter 22

Jack and his siblings decided to visit "White City Amusement Park". White City was just what its named conveyed. It was an amusement park for White Folks, which opened May 26, 1905 and it was located at 63rd and South Ave, which is now Cottage Grove in Chicago.

Jack, Baby Girl, Mary and Paul went to the amusement park. Jack had talked his siblings into going. Each of them was very light skinned and able to pass for white. Jack always wanted to venture to places that he didn't really need to be. He was determined to go, so they tagged along to keep him out of trouble.

It was a hot August day and cooler weather would be in Chicago before they knew it. It was Saturday around three o'clock. When they arrived at White City, it was extremely crowded. They paid the ten cents entrance fee and entered the massive crowd of White folks among the numerous rides and games. There were white buildings with strings of lights and the park covered fourteen acres. The buildings had been constructed with the feeling of Paris and painted in a chalky white. The park had lost a ballroom which held a thousand. It had been destroyed in a fire that past June, 1927. White City had seen better days with its gardens and strolling paths.

“Dees some mighty fine rides”, Baby Girl articulated. “Come ride dis rollercoaster wit me Jack. It'll be fun.”

Mary and Paul had no intentions of riding rides like the rollercoaster. They would ride on rides that stayed close to the ground and play the games.

Paul chimed in, “'You got duh heebie jeebies Jack?”

“Ain't got no jeebies. I's do bess wit my feet planted on the ground.” Jack barked loudly against the background noise of the park. “What y'all gonna ride?**”,** Jack asked Mary and Paul.

“We gonna play some games first; we might ride a few rides later”, Mary responded.

Jack announced, “How bout I stay wit Baby Girl, while she ride on some of dees rides. We meet y'all at the entrance at eight? ”

“Dis fine wit me”, Mary responded. “Me too” Paul responded displaying his agreement with Mary.

Baby Girl walked around the park picking out the rides of interest. Jack stood in line with Baby Girl for a few rides, but wouldn't get on. The amusement park was nice, but for the Negroes that worked there, it was a demeaning experience. These people experienced much heckling, racial slurs and threats from the white folks.

Jack planted himself on a bench, while he waited for Baby Girl to get off one of the rides. He looked up at the humongous rides in the parks and listened for screaming, cursing and folks spatting outlandish words from their months. He heard mostly noise and screams. Jack noticed broads with young'uns. There were three and four broads together with only one or two young'uns. He was starting to strategize how he could get himself in the company of some of these broads. He thought this amusement park might have some potential, if this was a place that attracted broads. Jack liked the broads. He didn't care what color skin they had.

Then he looked around and caught someone staring at him. This made him paranoid. He pulled his cap down on his head. Jack decided that this would be a good time to use the john. This time Jack didn't have to choose whether he would use the White Mens' john or the Colored Mens' john. This was White City. The johns in the park were for Whites only. The Color john was all the way on the other side of the park for the workers. When Jack returned from the john, Baby Girl had finished her ride.

“Dat was swell. I's can't wait tuh do dat again. You should try it Jack. Let’s get on dat ride over dhere.”

Jack replied, "Let's play some of dees games."

Jack was more paranoid than ever. He kept looking around and started turning around in circles. At one point, he was even walking backwards. He quickly figured out that walking backwards was not a good idea, based on the attention that he was drawing. He didn't want people to think that he had gone *mad*. He might get locked-up in an insane asylum, which wasn't much different from being locked-up in prison, either way, you locked-up.

Baby Girl asked, "What's wrong wit you? Why you acting like you done gone mad? Dees folks don't know we ain't white. We'd be dead by now; just don't go do or say nothing stupid. Just mind yo own potatoes and everythang be okay."

Jack purchased some game tickets, which costs two to five cents each. They played a milk bottle game, which included some hoops and a game throwing balls at a milk can. They played each of these games several times. Then they ran into the "Dunk the Nigger" game. They were appalled by this game and refused to play. The White Folks were having big fun playing it. There were long lines for these tanks and several of them. The Negroes working the dunk games had to tease the White folks and entice them into play. These games were revenue for the Negroes, even though they were very degrading. These Negroes needed to feed their families. They were probably paid, based on the dunks they received, which was based on how much they could lure the white folks.

Then Jack noticed a cooling center. This is where they could get out of the sun. It was a tent. Upon entering the cooling center there was a lemonade stand. Baby Girl purchased lemonade for both of them and they took a squat, underneath a big tree on the backside of the tent. They sat there sipping on cool lemonade. Jack wondered how big the twins might be. He thought that they should be spatting some words by now and Earl should be walking. Jack wondered if Sheriff Rodgers had given up his search and if he would ever be able to return home to Mississippi. He didn't want to live the rest of his life hiding. He wanted to take his niece Ella out places and not be concerned that he might be seen by some Cracker that he knew. Then he would need to pretend that she was some servant and this would never due. He was disturbed about losing his identity. *He was now Wade Johnson, a peckerwood from Georgia.* The thought of this pissed him off. He had mixed emotions and being at White City wasn't helping any. Baby Girl pulled him back from his deep thoughts.

"I wonder where Mary and Paul at? I hope dey okay. I'm glad Charles not here. I'm getting kind'a tired a Charles. He just not the man fo' me."

“I'm sure Paul and Mary fine. Dey been playing dis *White* game much longer dan us.”

“Yeah, but Mary ain't played it in a long time, being married tuh Jake an all.”

“So you gonna kick Charles tuh the curb?”

“I'm gonna have tuh, if he don't stop being so attached tuh his mama.”

Jack finished his lemonade and pulled out his pocket-watch. “It's almost eight o'clock. We's need tuh head towards duh gate.”

Chapter 23

Baby Girl retrieved Jack from the boarding house one Saturday afternoon in September. They hopped a motor bus over to South Park Boulevard in order to pay Charles a visit. As they rode the motor bus, Baby Girl expressed her frustrations with Charles.

"Charles just too attached tuh his mama. I's don't want no man dat can't do nothin' wit'out his mama's approval and agree wit everythang I say. He don't never have an opinion bout nothin'."

Jack realized that he had forgotten his hat. This caused him paranoia. "Damn it, I's forgot my hat. You come'a rushing me. What's burning yo britches? Charles know you coming?" Jack started running his fingers through his hair and became fidgety. He had become accustom to wearing something on his noodle. He had a feeling of nakedness. Jacks' hats served a certain amount of security.

After a forty minute ride, they arrived at a gray-stone duplex housing unit on South Park. Baby Girl knocked on the door. Charles's mother answered.

Ms. Hattie was a tall woman of thick built and sandy complexion. Her salt and pepper hair rather coarse and only partially hot combed. Ms. Hattie definitely wore an interesting hair duo.

"Lucinda, Jack, come on in. Charles said y'all be stopping by. He in dhere snoozing. Jack, I ain't never seen you wit'out somethin' on yo noggin."

This comment put Jack's paranoia over the top. He walked over to the window and started gazing out. Jack was a little-ticked at Baby Girl for rushing him out of the boarding house. Baby Girl could be pushy when her mind was set on something.

Baby Girl responded, "Ms. Hattie, I's guess'n Charles a little tired."

"Yeah Baby, dey working him hard at the hotel. It's been a while, since I's seen you Jack. How's thangs been?"

"I's doing just dandy Ms. Hattie. Everythang going well."

Hattie was no stranger to either one of them. Baby Girl had been dating Charles for about nine months now. Hattie knew the entire family, Jake, Mary, Ella and Paul. They met at a picnic sponsored by Ms. Hattie's church. Charles had invited the entire Brewer clan. Jack had actually been in Ms. Hattie's company on several occasions, since he spent so much time with Baby Girl. Ms. Hattie adored Baby Girl and hoped for a marriage, before the year was over. Baby Girl had no interest in marrying Charles and she didn't want Ms. Hattie for a mother-in-law.

Ms. Hattie commented, “Let me wake my baby. He been sleep long enough.”

Charles entered the room rubbing the sleep out his eyes. “Dat was some good sle'ap. Hey Jack! How's my gal doing?” Charles kisses Baby Girl on the cheek. He conveyed that business was well at the Palmer House, which had proven to be financially beneficial for him. “Y'all hungry? How's bout we get some viddles down here at the diner on the corner. I's done worked-up an app'tite.”

Baby Girl responded, “I's just got off from work. I grabbed some viddles at the diner. Jack not hungry. We just stopped by tuh pickup dat package.”

Jack didn't know why Baby Girl had said that he wasn't hungry. He was starving, but he played along with her, since she had expressed that she wanted out of this relationship.

Baby girl hadn't eaten either, but she didn't want to eat with Charles. She needed to tell Charles that their relationship was over and that he just wasn't the man for her.

Charles reached for a package laying on the table. He handed it to Baby Girl. She smiled graciously, as she handed him some dough. She didn't want to alert his senses that something might be wrong. This was another one of Baby Girls talents, besides for jigging and singing. She was also an extraordinary actress. There absolutely had to be a place for her in Hollywood.

Chapter 24

Bessie arrived in Chicago, the third Saturday in October, totting all the young'uns. Jack had to work, so Baby Girl met them at Union Station. When Baby Girl arrived at the station, there was a mysterious aura. She sensed that something bad had happen, but didn't know what.

She sat patiently among the crowd thumbing through a discarded newspaper. Then Baby Girl heard the announcement that a train from Iowa had derailed. The Station went into an uproar. The folks waiting for the Iowa train sent the station into an auditory sensation of no return. Folks were scrambling for information about the derailment. Baby Girl started thinking pessimistic thoughts about Bessie and the young'uns. "What if dey don't make it? What I'm gon'na tell Jack?" She calmed herself down with a short prayer and thanked the Lord that it wasn't the train from Mississippi. Baby Girl took a deep breath, exhaled and pushed out a walloping breeze from her diaphragm. Fifteen minutes later an announcement was made that Bessie's train had arrived. All her negative thoughts vanished.

She located Bessie with her hands full from the young'uns. Bessie was carrying Earl in her left arm and wedged against her left hip. The twins were trying to tug away from Bessie, but she had a noose tied around their chest. The bonding of one arm and shoulder from each of them, prevented extensive tugging, but it also gave them the appearance of Siamese twins. The noose tightened with every tug. Earl's visual perception appeared as though he weighed a ton and he had the nerve to have his thumb wedged between his lips.

“Bessie, over here”, Baby Girl tried shouting over the noise. She soon realized that this was a waste of her time and quickly made her way through the crowd.

“Where's Jack and what's the beef wit dees folks?” Bessie inquired

“He couldn't get off from work today and a train from Iowa went off the tracks.”

Chapter 25

Jack, Bessie and Earl were forty-five minutes late for Sunday dinner at Mary's. Baby Girl had kept the twins, Alec and Eddie overnight. When Jack, Bessie and Earl arrived, Jack immediately started playing with the twins. "Dhere's my boys; come tuh Papa." The twins didn't know quite what to make of Jack. They didn't know him. They ran straight for Bessie. Jack's face drooped into a slight frown, but he bounced back quickly and snatched the twins up, placing them on a knee, as he made himself comfortable in the rocking chair. Alec looked up at him with inquisitive eyes. Eddie pulled at Jack's hat, which he had forgotten to remove, during his excitement for the twins. Jack placed the hat on Eddie's head. "Give Papa a hug", pointing at himself and smiling from ear to ear. Eddie stared at Jack for a few seconds and smiled, so Jack gave him a hug.

Jake chimed in, "Lets get some viddles. Y'all late and I's starving."

Ella placed a very small wooden table, handcrafted by Jake, parallel to their table for Alec and Eddie. Wooden crates helped the twins plant themselves at the small table. Jack and Bessie sat together at the family table with Earl in the middle. The combination of Jake's carpentry skills and Mary's sewing skills had merged once again. They managed to create the cutest booster seat for Earl to use.

Mary was experiencing some fatigue from her busy week. Jake and Paul were ready to start stuffing vittles in their mouths, while Ella was getting her ears tuned-in for grown-folks' conversation. Jake led them in a prayer and they all dug in.

Seated across the table from Bessie was Baby Girl. She wanted to know how things were back home. "How my Papa doing? He managing okay wit'out me? Dat Sheriff still givin' y'all a hard time?"

"Papa Brewer doing fine. He mis y'all a little bit, but he won't admit it. He still a stubborn old mule. He took on a couple mo' sharecroppers. He send y'all his love. Everybody send dey love. James and Norman doing better now. Uncle Lonnie came tuh visit Papa Brewer last month. Mama Bertha had her hands full wit Uncle Lonnie being dhere. Dat Sheriff Rodgers dun calm down some. He ain't been snooping around so much. I thank he carrying a torch for a gal over on Beat 4. I thank her name Susie May. We not seeing much'a him dees days. I run into him at the market a couple times. I's show glad Earl look like me. Dat Sheriff be givin' me the eye like I's might know where Jack is. He can look all he want. I's ain't telling him, nothin'. Besides, dees young'uns keep me so busy, I's don't have time fo' nothin' else.

Where Charles at? Y'all still court'n'?"

"Charles had somethin' tuh do fo' his precious mama today. He too much of a mama's boy fo' me. We ain't been spending much time togetha. I'm glad thangs dun setdled down back home. I's been thanking bout paying Papa a visit. Mary, maybe you's can go wit me?"

"We'd need tuh go soon, if we going. I'll be busy making holiday clothing soon. I's got bout three mo weeks, befo' I's can't get away."

Earl was ready to get down from the table, so Jack placed him on the area rug that stretched across the wooden floor. Earl was actually walking well for a one-year-old and displaying great motor skills. Jack thought he was a chip off the old block, even if he did resemble Bessie.

Paul commented, "You's serious bout dis trip Baby Girl? I's might try and go wit y'all. I ain't seen Papa in a few years. It be good tuh see him and the rest of the family."

"Papa wouldn't know what tuh do, if all three'a us show up at the same time" Mary uttered out of her wore out body. "Me and Paul together....might cause him tuh have a heart-attack."

Jack chimed in, "I's know what he'd do. He'd make Norman roast a pig fo' y'all and James play the harmonica. Den he'd break out the hooch."

Jake changed the subject. He knew that his wife wasn't going South, unless Papa Brewer died. Mary couldn't stand the South. He muffled a few words from his stuffed mouth. "Jack, what y'all gonna do why Bessie here?"

Jack responded, "I seen somethin' in the Chicago Defender bout Sammy Stewart being at the Metropolitan Theatre. Dey say he got'a Orchestra dat play real nice. I's thought we'd catch a movie and listen tuh dem play. Dey play background music for the films. The theatre right here on 46th South Parkway. White folks still come over here, even though its predominantly us. Dey got all white workers at dis theatre. Dey had tuh brang the *NAACP* in, not too long ago. Dey what'n treating us right, but now dey gotta Colored manager. What you thank Bessie? How dis sound?"

Bessie responded, "Sound like we gonna be putting on the Ritz."

Mary commented, "Bessie, I's got somethin' dat'a fit you nicely, if you's didn't brang nothin' tuh wear."

Ella eased a few words into the adult conversation. "Aunt Bessie, how long y'all staying?"

"We's gonna stay until Thursday. Jack got's tuh work. He can't get off right now. Dey busy at the Mill."

Baby Girl volunteered to watch the young'uns. "I's working the breakfast shift at Larry's, but I's can watch the young'uns while y'all out. Y'all go out and have a good time. Ella be glad tuh help me wit the young'uns." She turned and winked at Ella, who was seated at the other end of the table.

They removed themselves from the table and gathered in the front room. Paul got a piece of Jake's wood out of the barrel by the fireplace. He pulled out his pocket knife, lit a cigarette and started whittling. Mary lit a cigarette too.

Chapter 26

Jack took Bessie out on Tuesday night to the Metropolitan Theatre. When they entered the theatre, it was somewhat crowded and filling up fast. There appeared to be a couple hundred Coloreds in the theatre this evening. It was a king-size theatre with plush red velvet seats. Sammy Stewart and his Orchestra were already pleasing folks' ears with their music.

Jack and Bessie were escorted to the Colored section in the balcony and seated in the middle of the first row. Jack wanted to sit at the end of the row, by the aisle. They quickly changed their seats. Jack was aware of his surrounding. There were too many white folks. He lived with white folks at the boarding house. He worked with Whites and Coloreds. Everyone at the steel mill thought he was White. He stayed away from the Coloreds at work, for fear of blowing his cover. He hadn't been to the boarding house in a couple of days, so he didn't know what was going on there. Jack had the possibility of being recognized and wanted to be seated where he could move swiftly.

Jack told Bessie, "Dis place hold 1400 folks and Sammy Stewart from Ohio. He been playing in Chicago for a while now. Dey the first colored orchestra to come to Chicago."

Bessie responded, “Dis sho is a fine establishment. Look how large dis place is. I thank the ceiling in here higher dan the one at the Earl Theatre.”

“Earl Theatre right down the street. We ain't took dis theatre over yet, but we will. Look at all dees Colored folks in here and dey gotta Colored manager now. White folks having tuh do what a Colored man say. Dey won't be coming in our area much longer.”

The Metropolitan was featuring a musical drama film that was part-talkie titled “The Singing Fool”. It had been newly released by Warner Brothers. Sammy Stewart and his Orchestra played until the film started. They also played a little during the film, since the entire film wasn't a talkie. Jack and Bessie enjoyed the sweet music. Jack had fallen in love with Jazz since he came to Chicago and this orchestra music was like something they had never heard.

***

After a marvelous visit with her husband, Bessie, the twins and Earl departed for Mississippi on that following Thursday. Jack saw them off at the station. Jack was carrying Earl and Bessie held on to the twins, one holding each of her hands.

“Well, I guess dis is it. Dis y'all train right here. Bessie I really wish you'd ponder on moving up here tuh Chicago?"

"I'll thank a'bout it Jack. I'm a country gal. The city is a nice place tuh visit, but I's don't wanna live here. Plus, you's gonna have tuh make some changes..."

"I's know dat I'll have tuh make changes and I'm willing tuh do dis. My fam'ly mo import'n. I's love y'all."

Chapter 27

The winter was on the fast-track. It appeared as though Chicago might get snow for Thanksgiving. Paul's birthday was also in November, so the Brewer Clan decided to celebrate them together.

Jake, Jack, Paul and Charles were engaged in a crap game by the window, while Mary, Baby Girl and Ella got things together. Jack was losing the crap game, telling lies, joking around, and anything else that he could spill off his lips. Jack was always the life of the party. He was a party all by himself. This part of him had not changed, even though he was Wade Johnson, the white man.

"Shoot'um right....or dey gonna be wrong all night long" from the mouth of Jack, mister party man.

Mary and Ella had done a little decorating. Mary had made a nice cover for the dinette table out of a beautiful piece of butterfly fabric. Ella had created an exquisite vase from wallpaper and a bottle and filled it with yellow chrysanthemums. She placed them in the center of the table. Ella had also baked her uncle a birthday cake. Pound cake was her favorite; therefore, they would be having her favorite cake with homemade ice cream for dessert.

They all gathered around Jake's eight seated dinette table. Baby Girl had fried some catfish. She had also fixed spaghetti, a mixture of collard and turnip greens too, which were Paul's favorite and of course cornbread. They gave Paul his pocket-watch right after digesting dessert, which was Ella's cake and Mary's homemade ice cream. They had gotten the watch engraved with three names: "In loving memory of Narcissus, Jerusha and Earl." Narcissus had been their mother. Jerusha was their sister that had been killed by the white man and her body left in the family yard. Earl was their brother who had been killed by an adversary and pushed on to the train tracks.

Paul was so emotional about receiving the watch that tears flowed from his eyes. Ella shouted, "Happy Birthday Uncle Paul". Jack started the party off by roasting Paul.

"Paul's ears so big, papa could call him home from Mis'ez Thompson's ten miles away."

After they finished roasting Paul, they told family stories which included their deceased siblings and Jake broke out the hooch. Mary told some stories about Paul, Jerusha and her when they were kids. Jack told some stories about how Baby Girl and he use to make Earl mad.

"Remember the time we caught Earl napping and put molasses in his hair". Jack stated with great admiration.

Baby Girl gave a giggling response, "Yep, I's remember. We's had tuh run and hide in the cotton fields."

Mary chimed in, "Paul you's remember when Jerusha was taking dat skin-dip in the pond and we snagged her clothes?"

"I's show do. She was mad at us fo'a month. I's was a little scared too. I's just knew she was gonna do somethin' tuh us. I's couldn't sleep at night."

They had some good laughs reminiscing about the olden days. Charles, Jake and Ella just laughed along as they continued sharing stories from back home. Charles was trying to snuggle-up with Baby Girl, but she wasn't having it. She had already decided that she wasn't going into 1928 with Charles. He was not the man for her. She was pained by his presence.

Jack started spacing out, losing his concentration. Baby Girl sensed that something wasn't right and inquired. "Jack, you done got quiet. Somethin' on yo mind? You gotta beef?"

Jack was upset about the letter that he had received from Bessie. He could almost act as well as Baby Girl, but not quite. He had a wrinkle in his forehead that became more noticeable when he got upset; he flicked his index finger on one hand. "Nope, ain't got no beef. I's had a bad week at work and dat bug going around. Dhere's a lot'a folks out sick."

The old tales went on for another hour, but Jack got more withdrawn. He eased himself away from the table and went to gaze out of the window. These old tales made him miss Mississippi. He thought about the old creek where he use to go fishing. He thought about Katie Cox. She was his first puppy love. Jack also reflected on the first time he took Duke hunting. Duke was the family hound dog.

Jake joined Jack by the window. They both stood there gazing out the window for a few minutes, observing the Christmas decorations that had started going up.

Jake asked Jack, "You's got a beef. You's standing over here by the window."

"I's got a letter from Bessie the other day. She knocked-up again. Dis make number four and she don't wanna move tuh Chicago. I's can't never go back home. I's guess I do have a beef."

"Everythang gonna be okay. Here have another drank". Jake

poured some more hooch in Jack's tin cup."

Jake put some music on the phonograph. They continued with their celebration a couple more hours and Baby Girl continued to be annoyed by Charles' existence.

Chapter 28

Baby Girl met Charles at their favorite restaurant two weeks before Christmas. She was all bundled up in her coat, hat, boots, scarf and gloves. The weather was nothing nice. She figured the least Charles could do was buy her a goodbye dinner for her troubles of putting up with him. She had been dating him for almost a year and it was time to get rid of Mr. Watson. Their relationship had gone nowhere.

As she came in close proximity to the restaurant, she could see Charles sitting by the window. He was thumbing through the newspaper and had that silly grin on his face, which he always had. She found this to be rather amusing, seeing that he could only read a few words.

When Baby Girl entered the diner, Charles stood up with great adoration. The diner was well lit and quite busy for a Wednesday. They sat at a table for two. It was a small soul-food restaurant and catfish was their specialty. Baby Girl loved some good catfish and she didn't feel like cooking. They didn't make very good catfish at the diner where she worked. She couldn't meet Charles there anyway, since Mr. Calhoun thought she was white folk and dating a Colored man would make him a *dead man*. She didn't want him anymore, but she didn't want him dead.

“How's my little dumpling today?” Charles leaned forward to give Baby Girl a kiss on the smacker. She quickly turned her head to the left and down.

“You's got a beef”, Charles pronounced with much concern.

“Let's just order some viddles. Mr. Calhoun been working me hard over at the diner and I's got some thangs dat I been pondering on. I'll have the catfish.”

“Well, I's gonna have the catfish too.”

This was one of the many things that Baby Girl hated about Charles. He made everything so easy. He agreed with everything she did, didn't do or said. She really couldn't stand the fact that he couldn't or wouldn't do anything without Ms. Hattie's approval. He was a grown man, but a mama's boy. Baby Girl had wasted enough time with him. She was a woman in need of a husband and on her way to being a spinster, unless she kicked Charles to the curb. She needed a husband. Not a man living with his mama, just because he didn't want to move out.

The waitress came to the table and took their order. Baby Girl was a little nervous. She sat there picking at her nails and flopping her right hand against her right cheek. Charles was really becoming concerned about what was on her mind.

"You's can tell me what's beefing you. Maybe I's can help." Charles said as he looked Baby Girl straight in the eyes, with that silly grin on his face. He had gotten a haircut and looked rather sheik. His big black eyes were piercing her soul. The waitress returned with their vittles and they began to eat.

"Charles, I's can't be yo gal no mo. I's not happy wit dis relationship. You's a little bit too attached tuh yo mama for me. I's sorry, but you's just not the man fo' me."

Charles was shocked and dumbfounded, after all this time that they had been courting. His dark skin even appeared a little red, due to him becoming so upset. He thought Baby Girl was fond of him, and his mother. His mother had an affection for Baby Girl. He had even pondered asking her to marry him. His mother was looking forward to a wedding. Charles was a scorned man.

"Well, I'm not gonna sit here and beg you tuh stay wit me. If dis the way its gotta be..."

He reacted just the way Baby Girl knew he would. Whatever she wanted to do was okay with him. Charles got up and left the diner huffing and puffing. He threw some money on the table for the vittles and hit the pavement. Baby Girl was relieved that it was over. A weight had been lifted off of her shoulders and a half smile came upon her face. The relationship with Charles had ended and not a moment too soon. She didn't have to bring 1928 in with Charles Watson. She was a content woman now, but Charles was heartbroken, so he went running home to tell Ms. Hattie.

***

“Mama, Lucinda jus broke-off wit me. She say I's ain't the man for her. I's too much of a mama's boy. She say she need a real man.” Charles started sobbing all over Ms. Hattie's shoulder.

“Oh, she did. Get hold of yo self now. It's gonna be okay. You know mama always take care'a thangs.”

Ms. Hattie was furious inside. She really liked Baby Girl, but tossing her boy to the side like this after all these months, would not be tolerated. Who did Baby Girl think she was? Hattie figured that Baby Girl thought she was too good for Charles. She was going to show this uppity light skinned Negro woman about messing over her son.

Charles didn't have any more contact with Baby Girl, after that day. Baby Girl was already moving forward and checking the market for a new man. Charles was brokenhearted and love sickened. Hattie watched him mope around the apartment. She had to do something.

Chapter 29

Baby Girl had to work at the diner Christmas Day, so the Brewers celebrated Christmas Eve at their usual spot around two o'clock. This was their first Christmas together as adults. Mary and Paul were so much older than Jack and Lucinda that they hadn't really shared any Christmases. The prior Chicago Christmas had been hit by ten inches of snow and Jack had stayed at the boarding house.

They all believed in having a big feast. Mary and Baby Girl had prepared favorite dishes. There was peach cobbler for Paul, bread pudding for Jack, blackeyed peas and cornbread for Jake and pound cake for Ella. These were just some of the fixings that Mary and Baby Girl had cooked. They had spent part of the night and all morning preparing for today's celebration.

The house had been decorated by Ella. She had drawn cute pictorials of snowmen, snowflakes, presents and of course Santa Clauses. These pictures hung around the doorways of the apartment. Ella had used some of her mom's fabric scraps to give them that holiday feeling. There was a beautifully decorated pine tree in the corner of the front room. The entire apartment had that fresh pine smell.

Baby Girl articulated, “I's glad to be rid of Charles. He had started making me unhappy. I's just couldn't stand tuh be wit him any longer."

Mary responded, "I's kind'a miss Charles. He was good for helping wit the viddles, seeing dat he worked in the kitchen, at the hotel. He set a table nicely."

"Dat's bout all he was good for." Baby Girl stated like a woman that was definitely tired of a man.

Jake chimed in, "Jack what you's got plan for New Year's?"

"Nothin'. Just gonna hangout at the boarding house. We's probably gonna get some snow. I's thank we gonna have a lot'a snow dis year."

"I's hope not", Jake commented, "The snow slow down construction and dis mean my carpentry work slow down."

Ella handed everyone their Christmas stocking. "Here you go Uncle Jack."

Jack checked his stocking out. He had received a new straight blade razor for shaving, with a nice stone handle. "Dis is nice. I's can really get a good shave now. I's thank y'all."

Baby Girl received a silver link bracelet with different colored glass-stones inserted in each link. Mary got a beautifully carved wooden brooch that had been hand painted in multicolor and trimmed in leather.

Paul and Jake's stockings also held straight blade razors. Ella had picked out the gifts for all the stockings.

"Ella, you got all the men the same thang?" Mary barked. Ella let out a big giggle and they all started laughing.

They had a nice Christmas Eve. Baby Girl fell asleep on the couch. They talked a little longer and ended their celebration.

***

Jack made his way back to the boarding house. When he arrived at the house several boarders were lounging around the house. Jack politely started to make his way to his room. One of the boarder's, Edward O'Reilly called out to Jack as he sauntered down the hallway "Hey Wade, Wade....". For this brief moment, Jack had forgotten that he was going by the name Wade and didn't respond to Edward O'Reilly.

Chapter 30

Ms. Hattie decided that there was only one way to get back at Baby Girl, for what she had done to her darling Charles. It was Monday morning and a brisk Chicago February day. Ms. Hattie was on her way to work, but she traveled a different route this morning. She was all bundled up and prepared to do what needed to be done. Hattie didn't do much to her hair. Her hair duo was always half-afro and half-straightened, so wearing a hat was a good thing for Ms. Hattie. She was dressed in her hospital uniform underneath her coat. She worked at Michael Reese Hospital on South Parkway Boulevard emptying bed pans. This is the same street that she lived on. The motor bus would take her straight down to the hospital and she could get there in thirty minutes. She ventured off the bus this morning at 35th Street, before reaching the hospital on 29th. This put her on one of the cities dividing lines between the Whites and the Negroes. Ms. Hattie had left the house in plenty time to get to work. She left three hours early. Ms. Hattie took a deep breath, got of the motor bus and proceeded inside the 4th District Police Station.

Ms. Hattie knew all about Jack and his troubles in Mississippi. Baby Girl and Charles dated for a year. Baby Girl was rather fond of Charles and a little smitten at the beginning of their relationship. Charles had spent a lot of time with Baby Girl and her family. She had told him all about the shootout and the sheriff. He knew Jack was passing for white at his place of employment and the boarding house. He also knew that Jack was using the name Wade Johnson. This was the name that Baby Girl used when she first introduced them. Ms. Hattie had gone on picnics with the Brewers. Plus, Charles told his mama everything.

Hattie decided that it was time to turn Jack into the authorities. Baby Girl had done Charles an injustice. It was time to get revenge on these light skinned Negroes passing for White folks.

Chapter 31

The Chicago Police Department investigated Jack regarding Hattie's complaint. They found him wanted by the State of Mississippi. Jack's whereabouts were given to the State of Mississippi, the State of Illinois and the Department of J. Edgar Hoover.

Two weeks after Ms. Hattie dropped a dime on Jack, there was a knock on the door at the boarding house. Mrs. Smith answered the door, peeking out over her cheaters. She wasn't big on church, so her Sunday morning's were spent reading the newspaper in the parlor.

“Oh my goodness! Officers, what can I do for you today? Is there a problem?”

There standing at Mrs. Smith's door, one Chicago Copper, one Illinois State Sheriff and one Federal Law Enforcer from the Bureau of Investigations.

The short stocky Federal Officer did the introduction, “Hello Ma'am, We've been informed that a Wade Johnson lives here. His real name is Eugene Brewer. He is wanted for a crime committed in the State of Mississippi. There's a warrant out for his arrest. Is he here?"

"Oh my goodness! Please come in. Yes, I do believe that Wade is here. I believe everyone is here today and the weather is dreadful. I saw Wade go out earlier, but I'm pretty sure that he has returned. I'm sorry. What did you say his real name is?"

"Eugene Brewer" the Federal Officer repeated. "He's a nigger that ran up here from Mississippi."

"A Nigger! Oh Lord! My Clyde is probably turning over in his grave. Please get him out of here. His room is right down that hallway. It's the third door on the left."

"Get the key Ma'am", the tall Sheriff stated with his deep commanding voice."

The house had a slumberous feeling, even though a couple boarders were lollygagging around the kitchen. Jack was in his room checking out the comic strips. Moon Mullins and Little Orphan Annie were his favorite. National Barn Dance was broadcasting on the radio. They featured comedy and country music. Jack had already been to Ethel's Place for his lucky breakfast, but they were out of buttermilk. He was intertwined with the comics and the radio. He didn't hear the unfamiliar voices in the house. This was one of those times, when Jack didn't need to be in Wade's world. He could just be himself and not have to pretend that everything was okay with the world. A couple boarders heard the Officers' voices. They had come out of their rooms.

Mrs. Smith returned with the key. The three law enforcement officers swaggered down the hallway. The Chicago Copper with his billyclub in hand. The Sheriff with his 38 Colt firearm drawn. The Federal Law Officer placed the key in Jack's door and turned the knob. The door flew open and startled the living day out of Jack. He damn near pissed on himself. He jumped up from his bed, wide-eyed and panic-stricken. The Chicago Copper yelled "Don't move and grab air Nigger." Jack's arms flew up like lightning had just struck him. All the color drained from his face. He broke-out in a cold sweat and a fluttering gut. He let out an articulated "Ho-o—ly Fu-uck". The Chicago Copper creamed Jack with his billyclub right across the side of his neck. Jack's body dipped-down, bracing itself against the bed. He nearly fell over. "Crap", Jack bellowed. There he was staring three officers in the face. The Sheriff had his pistol pointed at Jack's head. Jack was stupefied, as to how they had found him.

The weather was quite nippy outside for April. The officers allowed Jack to put on his hat, jacket and shoes. They didn't want him to get sick and die, before they could extradite him back to Mississippi for a proper southern punishment.

The handsome Chicago Copper grabbed Jack's coat, tossed it at him, but it fell on the floor. Jack didn't move. He didn't move because the Sheriff had his pistol pointed at him.

The tall Sheriff shouted, “Pick that up Nigger and get your hat and shoes on.”

The short stocky Federal Officer proclaimed, “Eugene Brewer, you're under arrest. There's a Warrant for your arrest in the State of Mississippi. We're taking you in. I've been sent here by the Bureau of Investigations to insure that you make it back to Mississippi. Put the bracelets on boys.” Jack put his hands behind his back and tears flowed profusely.

Mrs. Smith and some of the other boarders stood in the doorway watching. Word had already spread around the boarding house that Jack was a Negro. The boarders were chanting, “Get that Nigger outta here”. They clapped as the officers put Jack in constraints and moved him swiftly down the hall, out of the house and into the paddy wagon.

Jack was shaking his head and kept repeating “Damn”. He cried and cried and cried along with his repetition of “Damn, Damn, Damn”. His crying didn't taper any, until they put him in a Chicago cooler. He sat quietly in the cooler, feeling the end coming to his lives. His life as Wade and his life as Jack were both ending. Jack didn't want to go back to Mississippi. He definitely didn't want to go back as a captured Negro fugitive. There was nothing nice in Mississippi for a Negro, especially one that was accused of doing something against the law. The more Jack thought about returning to Mississippi, the more he cried. The worst his fears became and the more his anxiety heightened. He didn't want to be killed. He didn't want to die this way. Jack had been on the run for two years now. Mississippi wouldn't treat this lightly. He knew that Sheriff Rodgers would do everything within his powers to get retribution for Jack shooting his arm off, along with the killing of Alma Lark.

He closed his eyes and started praying to the Lord Jesus, with tears running down his cheeks. "Lord Jesus, please help me. I's sorry dat Alma Lark got killed, even dough I's didn't shoot her. I's sorry fo' leaving Bessie and the young'uns. I's sorry fo' not being around tuh help Papa wit the farm. I's sorry fo' cheating on Bessie. Lord Jesus, I's sorry fo' everythang I's ever done wrong. Please don't let me die. Ah'man."

There in a cooler, all by himself, Jack waited patiently to be extradited back to Lexington, Mississippi. He sat with his head in his hands, praying that everything would be okay. Death by

Hanging was definitely a possibility for Jack.

Jack was totally puzzled as to how they found him. He didn't have a clue that Ms. Hattie had turned him in. He figured that his family was unaware of his arrest. He knew someone would eventually come looking for him, but the question was when. He still had a week before his Sunday Dinner with his siblings. He would be in Mississippi or at least on his way by then. Jack might be strung up by his neck and never see his siblings again. His desperation caused a floodgate of tears to flow.

***

Back at the boarding house, Mrs. Smith was overwhelmed. She was upset with herself for harboring a fugitive. All nine boarders were out of their rooms and chatting among the house. Everyone was astonished that Jack turned out to be an imposter, except for an older hairless gentleman named Edward O'Reilly. Edward stayed in the room across the hall from Jack.

Edward commented to Mrs. Smith, "I knew there was something strange about that fellow. I didn't think his name was Wade. I was calling him one day from down the hallway and he didn't even turn around. That Southern accent didn't sound like Georgia, walking around with a cap on his head all the time. I knew something wasn't right with him."

Mrs. Smith was sitting at the dining table with a bottle of hooch and a cup. She could hardly sit up straight at the table. She sat patting her foot on the floor, shaking her head and tapping her hand on her thigh. Mrs. Smith was nervous, upset and mortified. "Clyde, Clyde, Clyde. Oh, I know he's turning over in his grave." She poured herself a stiff one and gulped it down, while reflecting on Jack's first Christmas in Chicago. Jack was one of several new boarders that came to live in the house. Mrs. Smith had made everything especially nice at the boarding house, during the holiday season. She had decorated and baked fresh cookies. She had even sat and drank hot ginger-cider with Jack. Mrs. Smith had treated Jack like he was her own son. She thought about the stories that Jack told on Christmas Day, about his adventures back in Georgia. They had all been lies. Jack had even helped her plant tomatoes in the garden out back. Mrs. Smith was shamefaced that she had been fooled by a Negro and poured herself another drink.

Chapter 32

Within a week, Jack was back in Mississippi. When papa John Allen Brewer got word that Jack was back, John Allen got in the Model T and headed for the Lexington jailhouse, which was about twenty miles away from Black Hawk.

It was the Wednesday after Jack had been extradited to Mississippi and around noon, when John Allen reached the Lexington jailhouse. Jack had been in Lexington, since that Monday. John entered the jailhouse with lots of conviction, as he politely nodded his head at the Sheriff. John Allen Brewer was a man of few fears. He was very focused and reeked determination.

“Good Afternoon Sheriff. I's looking for Eugene Brewer. Been told he's in the cooler here. I'd like tuh have a word wit'um, if I could?”

The jailhouse was untroubled. In the main room of the house sat three desks, along with one Sheriff and a Justice of the Peace.

The Sheriff looked up from his newspaper, which was being read from his large wooden oak desk at John Brewer dressed in his overalls. John looked like a white man, who had just finished a long ride in the hot sun. John removed a cloth from his pocket, wiping his forehead, while brushing back his slightly thinning hair.

The Sheriff skimmed his log sheet for Jack's name. "Eugene Brewer you say?" John nodded his head and replied with a no nonsense tone in his voice. "Yes Suh, dat be him."

"Willie, pat dis man down and take him tuh see prisoner eight", the Sheriff commanded to the deputy seated at the desk across the room, while he continued to analyze John Brewer from top to bottom. "You's got ten minutes."

There were several convicts locked in the coolers. The corridor was somber as John and the Deputy strolled to Jack's jail cell.

Jack hopped up from his cot, ecstatic when he saw his Papa. He stood there behind the dreary bars of the jailhouse cooler.

"Papa you's got get me outta here. I's don't know what happen. I was at the boarding house minding my own potatoes..."

The deputy stood there watching Jack and his Papa converse from a short distance.

"Don't worry, I's came soon's I got word. Good thang Mr. Jefferson still cleaning floors in dis here place. He done always looked out for our people. I'm gonna stay over here at Ms. Maebell's tonight. She usually keep a room for folks traveling from Black Hawk and Coila. I'll get up and go see Mr. Cage in the morning. He a mighty fine lawyer. You stay strong. Everythang gonna be okay."

"Yo time is up", the deputy announced.

Jack stood behind bars, watching his Papa disappear down the passageway. John Brewer glanced back at Jack with a determined look on his face. Jack hoped that he wouldn't be the third one of John Brewer's young'uns to die. He wasn't confident that his papa would actually be able to help him out of this situation. Jack was thankful that his family was aware of his circumstances, but still flustered about how the authorities located him. He traced his steps mentally, urgently seeking an answer to his captivity.

Chapter 33

When John Brewer arrived at Mr. Cage's office in Lexington, it was a one level structure with two front entrances. Mr. Cage shared the space with another attorney. John Brewer entered the door on the right with Mr. Cage's name. John was dressed in his finest black suit. He removed his fedora and asked the receptionist to speak with Counselor Cage. Mr. Cage was already conversing behind closed doors this morning.

"Ma'am, I's wondering, if I might be able tuh have a word wit Mis'ta Cage dis mo'ning? My name is John Allen Brewer. I's come from BlackHawk tuh see Mis'ta Cage."

"Mr. Cage is in'a meeting right now Mr. Brewer, but you can have a seat. I will tell him dat you are here, when he is free."

"Thank yuh"

John sat patiently in the waiting area with his fedora nestled in his lap. The waiting area was quiet and provided seating for three. No one else was waiting to see Mr. Cage this morning, so John forecast that he had a good chance of meeting with him.

The receptionist didn't have a clue that John Allen Brewer was a Negro. She offered him water. She offered him coffee along with some saltine type crackers. John politely refused all of her offerings and continued to wait patiently for Mr. Cage. Once Mr. Cage finished his prior business, a woman sashayed out of his office. The receptionist stepped into Mr. Cage's office and announced "Mr. Cage, There's a Mr. John Allen Brewer here to see you."

"John Allen Brewer?" Mr. Cage questioned with a puzzled face.

"Yes Sir, Mr. Cage. Mr. John Allen Brewer from BlackHawk."

"You may send him in."

When John Allen entered Mr. Cage's office, he was seated behind a beautiful wooden walnut desk. There were two exquisite wooden upholstered chairs on the opposite side of the desk. The windows were outlined with tapestry drapes and in the mist of this rich scenery sat a delightful little man named David Cage. He appeared somewhat ingested by his own desk. Mr. Cage was in his early forties. His hair was a dusky brown color, hinted with gray, but his heart was pure gold.

Mr. Cage accused John Allen of imitating a white man. John wasn't imitating a white man. He just looked white. The receptionist never thought to question his race, which was displayed in her hospitality. "Would you like some coffee or water Mr. Brewer?"

Mr. Cage professed, "John Allen, Why you walk in here like you a white man? You know damn well you not a white man! What brings you to Holmes County? How's the Misses doing? She still making them fine Blueberry pies?"

"I's never claim tuh be White, Mis'ta Cage. I just wanted tuh look presentable, when I's come tuh see yuh. The Misses doing mighty fine. I didn't know you's was fond of her Blueberry pie. I'll have Bertha make you one. I's came tuh talk wit you about my boy Jack. You might remember a shootout, he had wit one of the Sheriff's a while back. Dis happened a coup'la years back. A woman got killed in the crossfire. Well, dey found my boy up in Chicago. Done brought him back tuh Mississippi. Dey gonna put him on trial, here in Lexington. I's done already loss two of my young'uns, can't bare tuh lose another one. Jack my youngest boy. I thank you met him at the County Fair, a few years back. We'd be much obliged, if you'd help us. I'm not looking for no favors. I's can pay you. I just need a fine Lawyer like ya'self."

"Well now John, sounds like your boy done got himself in a pretty tough situation. This case may go to trial soon."

"Yes Suh Mis'ta Cage, but I'd be deeply appreciative, if you could find the time tuh represent my boy. Jack's always man'edg tuh find trouble, but he truly didn't mean for dat woman tuh get killed. Don't really know who shot'uh. She got caught in the crossfire, but Jack wasn't shooting in dat direction."

Mr. Cage agreed to take Jack's case, which thrilled John Brewer. Mr. Cage had established himself quite well, as an attorney in the State of Mississippi. John Brewer and Mr. Cage had done business in the past and things had always worked out well. John Brewer was convinced that Mr. Cage was the man for the job.

Chapter 34

It was Monday morning, nine days after Jack's arrest. Baby Girl knocked on the door at the boarding house. Jack had missed their monthly Sunday dinner. Mrs. Smith answered the door with a cup in one hand and her cheaters in the other hand. She was sipping noodle juice and giggle water out of her favorite cup.

“We--ll, I guess you a Nigger too? You-r bro-ther not here. They came and got him. Passing him--self off as White.” Mrs. Smith evoked with a slight slur in her voice and shaking of her head.

Baby Girl went into hysterics. “What you's mean, dey came and got him?” Her body-hair stood-up. The hair on her head, damn near stood-up. Baby Girl's mouth plopped open. Her eyes became bulged and her facial complexion couldn't decide what shade it wanted to be. All the nature curl damn near fell out her hair.

“Three off-i-cers came and ar-rested him last week-end. They said he was re--spon-si-ble for kill--ing some---body back in Mississippi. I am so glad they came and got that Nigger out of here. Now I have to replace every--thing in that room. No one wants to sleep in the same bed a Nig-ger slept in.” Mrs. Smith was feeling the giggle water, as it was apparent in her slurred voice. She continued sipping out of her cup, while Baby Girl articulated "Jesus Fucking Christ, Holy Shit". Then she ran off to catch the motor bus back to Mary's.

As Baby Girl rode the motor bus, she tried to figure out what had happened. How did the authorities find Jack? He left the South over two years ago. The last time Bessie came to Chicago, things had calmed down back home. Then Baby Girl thought about Ms. Hattie and Charles.

Hattie had threatened to turn Jack in several times, if Baby Girl broke up with her precious Charles. She knew it had to have been Ms. Hattie that dropped a dime on Jack. Baby Girl was steaming. She wanted to grab Ms. Hattie by her half straight, half nappy, salt and pepper hair and wring her neck like a chicken. She examined the folks on the bus, to see if Ms. Hattie was anywhere in sight. Baby Girl looked at each and every person that she could see without getting directly in their face. They could feel her wrath. It was like a swarm of bees had just been turned loose on the bus and everybody was being stung. Her look was so potent that the people riding the motor bus were scared to glance in her direction. She had infuriated written all over her. The folks on the bus didn't realize that they had an angry Negro sitting in the front. They thought Baby Girl was just some ticked-off white woman.

Chapter 35

Baby Girl told the family immediately about Jack's arrest, while packing her bags for Mississippi.

"Dat Mrs. Smith wit her drankin' self, say the authorities came and got Jack last week. Dis why he miss Sunday dinner. I's gotta get tuh Mississippi. I's know Ms. Hattie had somethin' tuh do wit dis. I's gotta get on the train. If I's see Ms. Hattie, I'm gonna be locked in the cooler. I's liable tuh kill dat woman."

Jake and Ella were trying to survive the wrath of the Brewer Clan. Mary started displaying agitation over the entire situation by taking her frustrations out on Jake and Ella. "Ella, didn't I's tell you tuh cut doz potatoes in small squares and put a pot'a water on. Jake, when you's gonna fix dis here shelf? Stuff falling all over the place." Spatting became Mary's native tongue.

Paul's annoyance was being taken out on Jake's wood. Paul was whittling it away. Together Paul and Mary filled the apartment with cigarette smoke.

***

Baby Girl got on the Pullman train back to New Orleans, which would stop in Greenwood, Mississippi. This was as close to home as she would get by train.

The train was half empty. Baby Girl rode in the white folks section on the train. She was sitting quietly in her plush velvet covered bench style seat, when a little boy appeared. He stood there for a moment staring at Baby Girl with his blonde hair and blue eyes. Then he spoke. “Why you so sad, Ma’am?”

Baby Girl had her arms folded in a relaxed matter, with a piece of tissue in each hand. She had been crying. She was staring out of the window when the boy appeared.

“Hello young man. Are you lost?” It was a long train and Baby Girl thought the young man had lost his way.

“No Ma’am, I'm not lost. Why you crying? Are you lost?” The boy's question about her being lost made her chuckle.

”No I's not lost. I's just so happy tuh be going home. I's been gone fo'a while and dees happy tears.”

The little boy smiled. “I's never seen happy tears befo’. Dey look just like sad tears.”

Baby Girl chuckled again. The boy's dialogue was just what she needed to lift her spirits. "Well young man, dey are definitely happy tears. I's should probably help you find yo seat. Yo mother is probably looking for you."

Baby Girl got up and strolled through the train with the young man. The boy had created a little light in her heart. She had been sitting there thinking about Jack and hoping not to find out that he was dead, once she got back to BlackHawk. She'd never be able to forgive herself.

***

Jack was sitting patiently in the cooler in Lexington, while Baby Girl made her voyage back to Mississippi. He was trying to feel confident that there would be a positive outcome. He was stronger and more composed, since his papa had came to visit. His family was now aware of the circumstances and hopefully help was on the way. Jack sat there staring at the ceiling, as he laid in his cot. He still had no idea what had brought his life to this point.

He asked himself, "Where did I go wrong? Who knew about my true identity?"

The only person that he knew about, that was aware of his identity outside of the family was Charles. Jack figured Charles must have something to do with his current situation and this meant it was Baby Girl's fault. Jack got mad at Baby Girl. He never cared much for Charles anyhow. Baby Girl was so smitten with Charles when she met him that Jack put up with him. Now Jack could be on Death Row, because Baby Girl had fallen in love.

Jack's face turned red and his fist tightened, as he continued staring at the ceiling. He knew it wouldn't be long before they put him on trial for the murder of Alma Lark and possibly be put to death. He opened his book "The Conquest: The Story of a Negro Pioneer" by Oscar Micheaux. The book had been delivered on behalf of the family, by way of Mr. Cage. Jack had to get his mind off of his current circumstances. The book was about Negroes coming to understand their potential and accelerating in areas that they had been excluded from.

Chapter 36

After traveling for twenty-four hours, Baby Girl had finally reached the Brewer family home. Norman and James were sitting on the porch. She had arrived by horse and buggy. You could rent a driver with a buggy at the train station to take you to your destination. "Why y'all just sitting dhere? Come over here and help me wit dees bags."

James spoke out, "We's didn't know it was you."

Norman pronounced, "My mind was somewhere else wit everythang dats been going. Dis might not be such a good place for you right now. Bessie and Papa both gotta beef wit you."

"Why? What I's do? I's ain't seen y'all in a year."

James responded, "Ain't you's the reason dey got Jack?"

They grabbed Baby Girls luggage and headed inside. Once they were inside the house, it was filled with the rattling of toddlers and adults. It was a sunny day and the sun beamed through the house. Bessie and the young'uns, Jack's stepmother Bertha and his oldest living sister Annie were all amongst the house. Bessie was sitting in the rocking chair in the front room, now six and a half months knocked-up.

The house had a huge front room with two couches, a rocking chair and a few other chairs for seating. There was a roomy size kitchen, with a dinette table and several bedrooms. Bertha was strolling around dusting and straightening up things. She was keeping herself busy, while trying to keep her mind off of Jack. Everyone was pretty much sitting around except for the twins and Earl, whom were playing. James grabbed a piece of wood and started whittling.

Baby Girl spoke, "How y'all? What's going on around here? I's came soon we found out what happened tuh Jack. By the time we's found out bout Jack, he had been gone fo'a week. Is he okay? Where is he?" The air in the room was thick. The only folks happy to see Baby Girl were the twins.

Bessie responded, "Jack in the cooler in Lexington. He suppose tuh go for trial next week."

"I's know dat gentleman caller Charles and his mama Ms. Hattie had somethin' tuh do wit dis. Ms. Hattie threaten tuh turn Jack in, if I broke-up wit her precious Charles. I's didn't believe she'd do it. I's knew dat woman was crazy. I's feel terrible bout the whole thang. I'm gonna see Jack tomorrow. Where's Papa at?"

Bertha responded, "John out in the fields. He's trying tuh keep his mind off'a Jack. He got dat lawyer Mis'ta Cage from Lexington tuh represent Jack. Dey might not let you see Jack at the jailhouse."

"Oh...I'm gonna see Jack! I's gotta see him. I's need tuh tell him what happened."

Norman chimed in, "He already figured out what happened. He was telling Papa what he thought happened. Jack gotta beef wit you."

Chapter 37

The following morning, Norman took Baby Girl to Lexington in the Model T Ford. After reaching the jailhouse, Norman decided that he would pickup a few things at the town store, while Baby Girl tried to see Jack.

There had been a disturbance at a local saloon and folks had been arrested, so the authorities were busy processing folks, due to property damages. Baby Girl had been dealt the card she needed. The business of the jailhouse made her acting performance a little easier.

One of the deputy sheriff's noticed Baby Girl as she approached. She sashayed over to the sheriff, with her form fitted red city dress that she had brought back from Chicago. She threw the officer a charming smile. “Sheriff, I's can see dat you busy, but I's here tuh see my brother Eugene Brewer.”

The sheriff knew Eugene Brewer was a Colored inmate, so he figured Baby Girl must be Colored too. Baby Girl's magical smile and glamorous looks, over powered any feeling that the sheriff had about Niggers.

“Eugene Brewer in the cooler, number eight. You see dat guard standing over dhere by the door? Tell him dat I said it was okay, for you tuh see number eight."

"I's much obliged Officer." She smiled graciously at the officer, as she strutted towards the guard, with hips swaying from side to side.

Between the chaos of the jailhouse and Baby Girl's highfaluting performance, the Sheriff had forgotten to search her, after experiencing such a spectacular performance.

When Baby Girl reached Jack's cooler, he was sitting facing the wall. "Jack it's me!" Jack turned around and looked Baby Girl in the eyes. He was happy to see her, but still upset with her, so angry that his tongue got stuck for a moment.

"Jack, please don't have no beef wit me. I's sure it was Ms. Hattie dat turned you in."

"Ms. Hattie!" Jack barked. He moved from the cot in the cell, over to the bars where he could speak more privately with Baby Girl.

"How Ms. Hattie know bout me? You's told her? You's spill everythang and now dey gonna kill me."

"I's didn't tell Ms. Hattie, but Charles tell his mama everthang. She threaten tuh turn you in, if I broke of wit her precious Charles. I's didn't really thank she'd do it." Baby Girl said with humility.

"Oh, you's didn't thank she'd do it?" Jack stated with the sound of astonishment.

"I's really sorry Jack. Please don't be mad at me. Everythang gonna be okay. Papa gonna take care'a thangs; he always do. I's come back, so I can do whatever I's can tuh help. I'll be in court every day." Jack just looked at Baby Girl dishearten.

"Yo trial start Monday. Dey might not let me see you again, but I's be in court every day, I's promise."

Jack leaped back over to his cot. He pulled out his book and commenced to reading. Baby Girl crept down the passageway with her head down, as the water leaked from her eyes. Her heart ached like it had never ached before. She hadn't only let Jack down, but her entire family. Baby Girl didn't know if they would ever forgive her, if Jack got sentenced to death.

Chapter 38

"All rise. Honorable Franklin Powers presiding," the bailiff broadcasted with a deep southern drawl. Your Honor was no ordinary judge. He was known across Mississippi as the Hanging Judge. A large framed gray haired man, with deeply creased wrinkles in his forehead, dressed in his formal black robe. His overall appearance expressed and agreed with his reputation of Hanging Judge.

Judge Powers placed himself at the bench and glanced over the courtroom, which was filled from top to bottom. Colored folks overflowed in the balcony. The main floor of the courtroom held about one hundred folks. There weren't any vacant seats on the main floor, which could only be filled by the Whites. They didn't know Jack or Alma. They were just present to see if another nigger would be killed.

"You may be seated", Judge Powers announced as he looked over his notes and gathered visual information on his courtroom.

Jack's verdict would not be decided by Judge Powers alone, but by a jury. This jury wasn't really in Jack's favor, because it was a jury of all-white-men. He did not have a jury of his peers. It was 1928 in Mississippi.

These men had been given the mission of deciding Jack's fate. Jack's defense attorney Mr. Cage was well aware of what they were up against. A Negro man on trial for the manslaughter of a Negro woman. Mr. Cage understood that this case wasn't about the death of this woman, but more about justice being served for a white sheriff who was shot in the arm by a nigger. As a result, the sheriff had lost his arm. Jack had really messed up!

Bessie was in the courtroom every day, dressed in her Sunday best. Papa John Brewer was present many days, supporting his family like he always did. Someone from Jack's family supported the trial daily. They took turns supporting: Baby Girl, James, Norman, his stepmother Bertha and some of his step-siblings. The family farm and fields still had to be worked and tended to. Sheriff Rodgers was also present in the courtroom.

There were twelve white jurors seated in the jurors' box. The Court Reporter was seated at a table between Judge Powers and the jury. The Reporter was a middle aged white male, with pen and pad ready to record the proceedings.

Jack felt somewhat naked without his fedora, which wasn't allowed on his head. He wanted to make eye contact with Bessie to reassure her that this was not the end of their life together. Bessie was seated in the balcony. Jack needed to look courtly, so he didn't pursue his desires of locating Bessie. His thoughts flashed back to the shootout and how everything happened so quickly. Jack realized that he wasn't the same man that fled Mississippi two years ago. He was a Negro man, who had lived and worked as a white man. He was now the father of three and a fourth young'un on the way.

The State Prosecutor was a man named George Crane. He had a great prosecuting record for his fifteen years, as an attorney. There were very few cases that he hadn't won. Mr. Crane was a short white man with beady eyes and ears that were too big for his head. He sat attentively at the Prosecutor's table, across the aisle from the Defense attorney Mr. Cage.

Judge Powers was ready to begin the proceeding. "Before us today, we have the Defendant Eugene Brewer. Mr. Brewer is being accused of Involuntary Manslaughter. Is the Defendant represented by Counsel today?"

Mr. Cage stood up. "Yes, your Honor. My name is David Cage from Holmes County. I will be representing the Defendant, Eugene Brewer, in this matter."

"Prosecutor Crane, Counsel for the State, are you ready to start the proceeding?"

"Yes, your Honor."

Folks started booing at the Prosecutor. Judge Powers immediately grabbed his gavel and started pounding it loudly against the sounding block. "Order in this Courtroom! This will not be tolerated in my Court." The spectators halted the booing and the Prosecutor proceeded with the case.

"This is a case of an innocent woman named Alma Lark that was trying to enjoy herself at a church picnic when Eugene Brewer, the defendant, decided to pick a fight with the Sheriff, whom happen to be patrolling in the area."

There was an elderly friend of Jack's in the courtroom. He gave a loud outburst, "Liar". Judge Powers banged his gavel hard against the sounding block and proceeded to have this man removed from the courtroom. "Anymore loud outburst and you will spend the night in jail"! The Judge gave Mr. Cage his chance to present his defense.

"Eugene Brewer is a victim of a crime, accused solely on the color of his skin."

The Judge didn't know quite what to make of this statement. He knew Jack was a Negro, but the color of his skin was that of a white man. Judge Powers told Mr. Cage to continue.

"Mr. Brewer is an innocent church goer. He was at a picnic with his family following a wonderful church service. They had just given praise a few hours earlier."

Folks in the courtroom on Alma Lark's behalf, started hissing and hooting at Jack's lawyer. A woman pitched a pebble in his direction, which landed on the Judge's bench. She was seized and thrown in the cooler for the night.

The Judge pounded his gavel fiercely on the sounding block. It took several hits and a few minutes to get the courtroom to calm down. "Order! Order! Order in this courtroom! If there is one more outburst of any kind in this courtroom, you will serve thirty days in jail!" Judge Powers was furious. They were about to find out, why he was known as the Hanging Judge. His face had turned red and his jaws were puffed, which left your imagination to produce the smoke coming from his ears.

All was calm and quiet in the courtroom. The trial continued. Prosecutor Crane was ready to call his first witness. "Fletcher Harris to the stand." Fletcher was a Negro man that attended Jack's church. Fletcher was sworn in by the bailiff, on the Negroes Bible.

“Do you promise to tell the truth, so help you God?” “I's do.”

“You may proceed Counselor”, Judge “Powers barked.

“Did you witness the defendant Eugene Brewer in a shootout?”

“Yes Suh, I did”

“Was Alma Lark killed in that shootout?”

“Yes Suh.”

Well, the Prosecuting Attorney produced several witnesses. They all stated that Jack had been involved in a shooting and Alma Lark got killed. These witnesses were produced within the first few days of deliverance. All of these witnesses had been bought, tortured or coerced by the Sheriff and his Klansman, into giving false testimonies against Jack.

Jack's blood pressure went up. He was sweating bullets and loosening his shirt collar. His fate was about to be determined by an all-white jury. Jack tried not to appear frightened, but he was scared out of wits. He prayed to Lord Jesus in his head. He looked around the courtroom and spotted Baby Girl. She was in the balcony. The balcony curved around the room. Baby Girl had positioned herself where Jack could see her, if he just looked up. She had a smile on her face, hoping that this would reassure him. Jack glanced up and noticed Baby Girl. He wanted to smile back at her, but he couldn't force a smile on his lips. His current circumstances were crushing all the life out of him.

After four days in court, it wasn't looking favorable for Jack. The trial days were long and exhausting. Counselor Cage was losing the case. The result could be Death by Hanging for Jack.

***

John Brewer got busy contacting his cousin Earl Leroy Brewer. Papa Brewer was determined to do everything that he could to save his son. John Brewer sent a telegram to his cousin, the Ex-Governor, Earl Leroy Brewer in Clarksdale, Mississippi. He explained the critical need for his assistance. Papa Brewer wanted justice for his son. He reminded Earl Leroy that Jack was family and Blood Is Thicker Than Color. He let Earl Leroy know that he needed him to do everything within his powers and that it wouldn't be right to just let them hang his kinfolk, without putting up a fight. He requested his appearance in court and provided him with all the details of the case.

Chapter 39

It was the second week of Jack's trial and the eighth day of proceedings. Photographers had started hanging around the courthouse. The bailiff appeared well rested, as he delivered an echoing "All rise. Honorable Franklin Powers presiding." Judge Powers took his seat at the bench, placing his cheaters on his piercing eyes. He gazed around the courtroom taking notice of everyone: Jack, the Jury, the Spectators and the Counselors. Then he stumbled upon a familiar face. It was Earl Leroy Brewer, the Ex-Governor of Mississippi. Judge Powers nodded his head slightly at the Ex-Governor, acknowledging his presence. Earl Leroy was seated to the right of Jack and Mr. Cage was seated to his right. Earl Leroy Brewer was more than an Ex-Governor of Mississippi. He was an outstanding attorney.

Seeing that family meant so much to Earl Leroy, he had accepted John Allen's invitation to help Jack. Even though Earl Leroy was white and John Allen was a Negro, there was blood between them and Blood Is Thicker Than Color.

Earl Leroy's most widely known case was the Mrs. Casey Jones of Jackson, Tennessee lawsuit. This was a suit against the Illinois Central Railroad over her husband's death in a train wreck at Vaughan, Mississippi. There is a famous engineer song and story about Casey Jones. Mrs. Jones was the Governor's most famous client during his career as an attorney. Casey Jones had a clever method of throwing his train into reverse and using it as a brake. This is where Casey Jones gained his reputation of being able to stop a train in much shorter space than most engineers.

From 1912-1916, Earl Leroy Brewer held the office of Governor. During his term in office, prisoners from the State Penitentiary came to work in the Governor's Mansion. These prisoners had life sentences and many of them were Negroes. This helped ease their incarceration time, especially those serving life sentences.

The first laws were enacted prohibiting children under the age of sixteen to work in factories in Mississippi. He also limited the hours that women and children could work. These laws were enforced with an inspector, who could see if they were being violated. The Governor was often criticized for using his pardoning powers. Earl Leroy Brewer pardoned more people during his four years in office, than any of the prior governors.

He gained some of his greatest notoriety when he aided and assisted Dr. Joseph Goldberger. An experiment was conducted at Rankin State Penitentiary, with thirteen volunteer white prisoners to determine the cause and cure for Pellagra. They were sworn to secrecy. The disease was called the "red death" of the south.

The doctor's theory was confirmed. Pellagra was caused by deficient diet. The Governor made sure that these people had volunteered for the testing and that the Negroes weren't used for this experiment. There was the possibility that people might die.

Governor Brewer had many political fights with his Lieutenant Governor Theodore G. Bilbo. The Lieutenant was a member of the Klu Klux Klan. Governor Brewer had to work side-by-side with Bilbo. The Governor was a man fighting for Human Rights and didn't get along with the Klan.

Chapter 40

It was time for the Prosecuting Attorney to give his Summation. "Gentlemen of the Jury, before you is the defendant Eugene Brewer. You have heard testimony from various people, who witnessed the killing of Alma Lark. She was shot down, trying to enjoy herself at a church picnic. You must sentence this man to death."

Earl Leroy delivered the Summation for the Defense. Earl Leroy Brewer introduced himself to the court and began his summation. "There will be no Hanging for Eugene Brewer." These were the first words out of Earl Leroy's mouth.

Earl Leroy Brewer was a tall man of big bone stature. His hair was fully gray with little depletion. Due to the Ex-Governor's presence, photographers hung outside the courthouse.

Judge Powers was curious. What was about to happen in his courtroom? He had an attorney named Brewer that was a white man and an Ex-Governor for the State of Mississippi. Then there was Eugene Brewer, the Defendant, a Negro fugitive on trial for manslaughter. They were both Brewers. They both looked White and the family resemblance was apparent. Judge Powers found this to be somewhat out of the ordinary. He showed a special interest in what Earl Leroy Brewer had to say, regarding this case.

Earl Leroy proclaimed, "Gentlemen of the Jury, I would like for you to take a good look at the defendant, Eugene Brewer. Does he look like a murderer? I would have to say no!"

Jack sat tensely in his seat, dressed in a fine black three piece suit. He managed to exhibit a slight smile on his face, when Earl Leroy pointed at him. Papa John Brewer wanted his son dressed in his Sunday finest. Someone from Jack's family took him a different suit to wear everyday of the trial. People couldn't tell whether Jack was the lawyer or Mr. Cage was the lawyer.

Earl Leroy continued, "Mr. Brewer is a hard working father of three children, with a fourth child on the way. He didn't set out to kill Alma Lark. Eugene Brewer found himself in a situation that caused conflict to occur between himself and a Constable. Yes, this woman was an innocent bystander. We mourn over her loss, but you must not sentence a man to death for merely being involved in a disruptive situation. The Defendant, Eugene Brewer and a Constable, were both engaged in gunfire. There has been no concrete evidence that my client's bullet killed this woman. I realize that you have heard testimony, but you must not be so quick to believe everything that you hear. Yes, the Defendant, Eugene Brewer, did flee the scene of the incident, but Mr. Brewer knew that he would be blamed, just because he is a Negro. The right thing to do is to set him free, so that he may return home to his family. He needs to be at home, where he can be a good father to his children. This is what they deserve. Don't sentence a man to death, based on the fact that he is a Negro."

There was another loud disturbance in the Courtroom. "Nig-gah Lover". The noise level escalated. Judge Powers pounded his gavel and stood-up. "Order in this Courtroom! Bailiff, remove that man immediately from my courtroom. Give him thirty days and start him off in the hotbox!" The courtroom got so quiet, Jack could hear his own heartbeat. Judge Powers was ready to hang somebody. "Now, does anyone else have something that they want to say in this courtroom today?"

By this time, Jack's handkerchief was soaked from his ceaseless sweating and his heart beat like he had just run several miles.

It was the Prosecuting Attorney's turn to give his rebuttal. "You have just heard the Defense state that this was merely an innocent mishap. It was a mishap that caused a life to be loss and a man to be left with one arm."

"I Object, your Honor! The defendant is not on trial today for anything other than the unfortunate death of Alma Lark", Earl

Leroy Brewer stated with conviction.

“Strike that statement from the record”, Judge Powers echoed.

The Prosecutor continued, “You have heard witnesses in this case. I urge you to consider the evidence carefully and deliver the correct verdict of Death.”

Judge Powers spoke, “You have heard all the evidence presented in this case. It is up to you ___the jury___ to come back with the correct verdict.”

The all-white jury went into deliberations. There was much concern about the outcome of this trial, causing stress among Jack and his family. Tension lingered over parts of BlackHawk and Coila.

***

Jack sat in the cooler perspiring, as he waited to be beckoned for his sentence. He gnawed at his nails, due to nervousness. He prayed day and night that this wouldn't be the end of his life. Jack yearned to be with his family and to be a free man once again. He felt great remorse over the death of Alma Lark, but he wasn't willing to die for a crime that he had not committed.

***

In two days, the jury was ready to deliver the verdict. Judge Powers entered the courtroom and sat in his chair on the bench. The courtroom was full of white folks wanting to know the verdict. Would this Nigger be sentenced to death?

Jack sat patiently between Mr. Cage and his cousin Earl Leroy, as Judge Powers sized up the appearance of his courtroom. The Judge sat up straight in his chair and took a sip of water from his glass. Then he spoke "Has the Jury reached a verdict?" The foreman for the jury stood up. He was a white man around thirty-five years of age, tall and lanky with dark brown hair. "We have your Honor. We find the defendant Eugene Brewer Guilty of Involuntary Manslaughter and sentence him to two years at Parchman State Penitentiary."

Somebody shouted, "Hang dat Nigger". Judge Powers immediately stood and started to sound his gavel, but the courtroom had quickly gone into an auditory level that required several minutes to regain control of.

Jack was relieved that he didn't receive the sentence of death by hanging. Tears of relief flowed from his eyes. He was still upset inside that he had gotten caught, due to Baby Girl's boyfriend, but he was content to do the two years in the State Penitentiary. A bailiff along with a sheriff escorted Jack out of the courtroom. Jack gazed up into the balcony making eye contact with Bessie, as they pulled him from the courtroom. Then he lowered his head and walked softly out.

***

Eugene "Jack" Brewer survived his two years at Parchman Farm State Penitentiary in Mississippi, with the help of his cousin Earl Leroy Brewer. Earl Leroy used his power and influence in the State of Mississippi to protect his cousin Jack, while he was incarcerated.

Sheriff Rodgers didn't feel as though he had received reparation for his missing arm. This meant Jack might come-up dead and Earl Leroy knew this, so he put the word-out. *"If one hair is missing off Eugene "Jack" Brewer's head, somebody gonna catch hell", because* BLOOD IS THICKER THAN COLOR.

Epilogue

Bessie was knocked-up once again, when they hauled Jack off to the penitentiary. She decided not to be married to a jail-bird and they were divorced by 1930.

Jack served his two years on Parchman Prison Farm and eventually returned to Chicago and started to live a normal life. He lived with the Black folks on the Southside of Chicago, remarried and remained in Chicago until his death in 1973.

Unfortunately, James was killed on Christmas Eve 1935, after gambling and having successful winnings. His family received the word of his death from a Sheriff on Christmas Day. This is what his children got for Christmas.

After Jennie and Wilbert moved to Missouri, Jennie started going by the name, Eatoy. Meanwhile, Baby Johnny grew-up. Wilbert grew to dislike him more and more. Johnny also grew to dislike Wilbert. Wilbert was a very angry man and was often abusive to Eatoy because Johnny had been born. Johnny and his siblings had to witness this abuse. They all hated him, even Wilbert's biological children hated him. As Johnny got older, he got to experience more of Wilbert's abusive behavior. Wilbert was always threatening to kill little Johnny, pointing his rifle at him and telling him that he was going to shoot him. By this time, Johnny was old enough to understand that Wilbert was not his dad.

Wilbert's temperament eventually got the best of him. He killed his two teenage neighbors for stealing from him. He received the electric-chair January 3, 1941 for this crime.

Johnny served in World War II and eventually moved to Toledo, Ohio, which is where some of his other siblings had already moved. Johnny eventually found out who his real father was from his stepbrother's wife. This occurrence happened while he lived in Ohio. He went to Chicago and met his father (Jack). Johnny also became in search of employment and found work in Chicago. He moved his family from Ohio to Chicago, where he resided until his death in 1987 and built a strong relationship with his father Jack. His mother (Jennie) remarried after Wilbert was put to death and she herself died in 1983.

John Allen lost his nine hundred-acres of land, due to women, alcohol, swindlers and wages not paid that were owed to him. He resided with Norman the last two years of his life and passed away in the earlier '50.

Norman continued to reside in Mississippi, married and had a family. He died in 2008.

Earl Leroy Brewer became known as a Civil Rights Lawyer, during his professional career. He did a lot for Negroes. One of his biggest cases was won before the U.S. Supreme Court. It was the Kemper County Trio case. This case involved three Negro boys who were beaten for five-days in the Kemper County jail, until they confessed to a murder. He charged no fee to represent these Negro clients and the court cost was paid by the National Association for the Advancement of Colored People (NAACP). The Kemper Boys did do some jail time, but they didn't get sentenced to death.

Earl Leroy died in 1942 in Clarksdale, Mississippi. He had a replica of the governor's mansion (Jackson, MS) made in Clarksdale. It is still standing today.

Baby Girl was portrayed in this story, so that she could help explain how Jack got arrested. Baby Girl is a fictional character and is no way a representation of any of his sisters.

Sheriff Rodgers is the fictional character who represents the real constable that Jack had the shootout with, but does not portray this person in anyway.

Jack did have a brother named Paul (Lanier), but not much is known about him or his life.

Mary, Ella and Jake were strictly fictional characters.

Charles represents the boyfriend that Jack's sister had in real life and Ms. Hattie represents the role that this man's mother played. Their actual names, personalities and characteristics are unknown, but they were responsible for Jack's extradition back to Mississippi.

All the characters in the book are fictional.

About the Author

TJ Morris started her artistic career as a student at Columbia College of Chicago and graduated with a B.A. in Liberal Arts. Already working in the medical field, she later became a Multimedia Artist for Medical Publications. After exploring more than 25 years in different genres as an artist, TJ found her calling in the world of writing. Publishing her first book of poetry in 2004 "The True Heart". TJ Morris never thought about writing, but after various ups and downs in her own life, she found herself writing a new chapter.

CPSIA information can be obtained
at www.ICGtesting.com
Printed in the USA
LVHW080713100719
623539LV00007B/471/P